AN ANALYSIS OF THE CIVIL LAW

IN WHICH

A COMPARISON IS OCCASIONALLY MADE

BETWEEN THE

ROMAN LAWS

AND THOSE OF

ENGLAND

BY

SAMUEL HALLIFAX, LL.D.

LATE LORD BISHOP OF ST ASAPH,
AND FORMERLY THE KING'S PROFESSOR OF THE CIVIL LAW.

A NEW EDITION WITH ALTERATIONS AND ADDITIONS

BEING THE

HEADS OF A COURSE OF LECTURES

PUBLICLY READ IN THE

UNIVERSITY OF CAMBRIDGE

BY

JAMES WILLIAM GELDART, LL.D.

THE KING'S PROFESSOR OF THE CIVIL LAW.

With a new introduction by

Michael Hoeflich

John H. & John M. Kane Professor of Law
University of Kansas School of Law

THE LAWBOOK EXCHANGE, LTD.
Clark, New Jersey

ISBN 978-1-58477-890-5

Lawbook Exchange edition 2008, 2022

The quality of this reprint is equivalent to the quality of the original work.

THE LAWBOOK EXCHANGE, LTD.
33 Terminal Avenue
Clark, New Jersey 07066-1321

Please see our website for a selection of our other publications and fine facsimile reprints of classic works of legal history:
www.lawbookexchange.com

Library of Congress Cataloging-in-Publication Data

Hallifax, Samuel, 1733-1790.
An analysis of the civil law : in which a comparison is occasionally made between Roman laws and those of England / by Samuel Hallifax.
p. cm.
Originally published: Cambridge [England] : Printed at The Pitt Press, by J. Smith, Printer to the University, for T. Stevenson, 1836. With a new Introd. by Michael Hoeflich.
Includes bibliographical references and index.
ISBN-13: 978-1-58477-890-5 (cloth : alk. paper)
ISBN-10: 1-58477-890-3 (cloth : alk. paper)
1. Roman law. 2. Civil law--Great Britain. 3. Law--Great Britain. I. Title.
KJA160.H35 2008
340.5'4--dc22 2008034192

Printed in the United States of America on acid-free paper

INTRODUCTION

Samuel Hallifax was born in Nottinghamshire in 1733 into a merchant family.[1] He matriculated at Jesus College, Cambridge in 1750, received his B.A. in 1754 and his M.A. in 1757. From 1756 he held a number of positions at Jesus including that of dean and tutor. In 1760 he moved to Trinity Hall, Cambridge, then the center of legal studies at the university where he served as a fellow from 1760 until 1775. During this period, Hallifax became an expert in Roman Law and also became deeply involved in the political and religious controversies of the day.[2] He, apparently, was both ambitious and not afraid of controversy. According to one account, an undergraduate threatened to shoot Hallifax because he felt that he had been slandered by him.[3] He not only held the Regius Professorship in Law from 1770 until 1782, but he also served as the university's Professor of Arabic, a language he didn't know, for two years.

Beginning in 1774 Hallifax also proceeded to hold a series of ecclesiastical position in the Church of England. He began as a royal chaplain, then became Rector of

---

1. Basic biographical facts on Hallifax are drawn from the article by Robert Hole in the new *Oxford Dictionary of National Biography* (Oxford: O.U.P., 2004).
2. See, D.A. Winstanley, *The University of Cambridge in the Eighteenth Century* (Cambridge: C.U.P., 1922), pp 281-290; John Gascoigne, Cambridge in the Age of the Enlightenment (Cambridge: C.U.P., 1988), pp.195-196; Henry E. Malden, *Trinity Hall* (London: Robinson, 1902), p. 205.
3. Winstanley, Op.Cit., n.3, above, pp.19-20.

Warsop in Nottinghamshire, then Bishop of Gloucester in 1781 and finally Bishop of St. Asaph in 1789.[4] During his lifetime he was better known for his religious writings than for his legal text.

Hallifax's *Analysis of the Roman Civil Law* was, in fact, based upon the lectures he gave as Regius Professor. He would seem to have begun to work on the lectures soon after he took up the Regius Chair.[5] The earliest version of the text was published at Cambridge in 1774 and continued to go through many editions until 1836.[6] The lectures, while reputed to be dry, were not unpopular[7] and the book made from them was widely distributed and continued to be used at Cambridge until the middle of the nineteenth century.[8] One can suppose that the success of the work derived both from a serious lack of competitors in English and from the relatively clear exposition and comparative approach Hallifax took in the

4.Hole, Art. Cit., n.1, above.

5.Hole, Art. Cit., n.1, above.

6. The first appearance of the work was titled *An Analysis of the Roman Civil Law compared with the Laws of England: being the heads of a course of lectures publickly read in the University of Cambridge*. The 1836 edition was edited by James William Geldart and titled *An Analysis of the Civil Law, in which a comparison is occasionally made between the Roman laws and those and those of England.*

7. Hole, Art. Cit., n.1, above.

8.A copy of the 1795 fourth edition in my own collection interleaved and filled with lecture notes taken by a Cambridge student in 1833, one Frederick William Hohler, of Trinity College, Cambridge.

lectures and book. The editor of the fourth edition of 1795 noted in the preface that, in this comparative approach, Hallifax had followed upon Cowell's *Institutiones Iuris Anglicani.*[9] An example of this comparative approach, for instance, is found in chapter nine: "Of Succession by Law." In this chapter Hallifax not only gives the legal rules of both Roman and English law, but also points out the differences. Such an analysis would have been of great use to his students.

To the modern scholar of Roman law, Hallifax's *Analysis* is more a curiosity than it is a useful textbook. It was written at a time before the great advances made by German jurists and legal historians of the nineteenth century. It was based, in large part, on editions of the primary texts which we no longer accept as authoritative. On the other hand, Hallifax's text is extremely important to legal historians who are interested in the development of law teaching in England and of the reception of Roman law in England and other English-speaking areas in the late eighteenth and early nineteenth centuries. It is also of great interest as one of the earliest comparative legal treatises produced in England and rightly takes its place in succession to Cowell's work.

Michael Hoeflich
July 2008

9. Samuel Hallifax, *An Analysis of the Roman Civil Law* (4th ed., Cambridge: Archdeacon & Burgess, 1795), p.v.

AN

ANALYSIS OF THE CIVIL LAW

IN WHICH

A COMPARISON IS OCCASIONALLY MADE

BETWEEN THE

ROMAN LAWS

AND THOSE OF

ENGLAND

BY

SAMUEL HALLIFAX, LL.D.

LATE LORD BISHOP OF ST ASAPH,
AND FORMERLY THE KING'S PROFESSOR OF THE CIVIL LAW.

A NEW EDITION WITH ALTERATIONS AND ADDITIONS

BEING THE

HEADS OF A COURSE OF LECTURES

PUBLICLY READ IN THE

UNIVERSITY OF CAMBRIDGE

BY

JAMES WILLIAM GELDART, LL.D.

THE KING'S PROFESSOR OF THE CIVIL LAW.

CAMBRIDGE:
PRINTED AT THE PITT PRESS, BY JOHN SMITH,
PRINTER TO THE UNIVERSITY.
FOR THOMAS STEVENSON, CAMBRIDGE;
AND
JOHN WILLIAM PARKER, LONDON.

M.DCCC.XXXVI.

THE LAW OF ROME HAS THE DISTINGUISHED HONOUR OF VINDICATING TO ITSELF THE EXCLUSIVE TITLE OF "THE CIVIL LAW"

ADVERTISEMENT

TO THE PRESENT EDITION.

In publishing a new edition of the Analysis of the Civil Law, I deem it right to declare that I have accustomed myself much to admire the arrangement and execution of Dr Hallifax's work. The reader is therefore requested to observe that the alterations and additions which have now been introduced are chiefly such as circumstances seemed to require. My design has been not so much to enlarge the text as to present it in such a form as would render my Lectures more useful and instructive, rather than more elaborate.

In adding the names of various authors for the purpose of reference, I have made a selection of those only which are required to put the student in full possession of the subjects of the Lectures. Many others I might have added, but I am unwilling to discourage the student by an array of books which he may not have time and opportunity to peruse.

It has ever been my object to support the honour and dignity of my Faculty, and in promoting the study of the Civil Law, I trust that I am contributing to the interest and reputation of the University.

J. W. G.

CAMBRIDGE, 17*th May*, 1836.

PREFACE

BY Dr HALLIFAX.

It is no small recommendation of the Roman Civil Law, as it was reformed in the sixth century after Christ by the eastern Emperor Justinian, that the general principles of it are delivered *systematically*. In the Digests, Code and Novels, which contain the responses of the Roman lawyers and the constitutions of the Roman emperors, an exact and methodical distribution is not always strictly regarded; but another work was prefixed to these, and confirmed by the authority of an imperial sanction, in which the elements of jurisprudence are disposed in a didactic form, its chief and leading objects are explained in a regular series, and the whole arranged in such a way, as neither to oppress the student with a multitude and variety of matter, nor yet to leave him destitute of any necessary helps to facilitate his progress in legal knowledge[1]. No such treatise is extant concerning the laws of our own country; and even the Commentaries of Mr Justice Blackstone, excellent as they are, are still but the work of a private man, and without the stamp of public authority.

The book here alluded to is commonly known by the name of the Institutions of Justinian; which, as the proemium to them sets forth, were composed in order to teach the *rudiments of law*, and were divided so as to contain the *elements of all legal science*[2]. This book, together with such portions of the Digests and Novels as were necessary to make the system of Roman Law complete, it is the business of the following Analysis to unfold: and whatever other defects are to be found in it, and however ill the design itself may be executed, one advantage at least it is sure of, which in such a treatise is far from being inconsiderable, that it is planned after the best model.

[1] *Incipientibus nobis exponere Jura Populi Romani, ita videntur tradi commodissime, si primo, levi ac simplici via, post deinde, diligentissima atque exactissima interpretatione, singula tradantur. Alioqui, si statim ab initio rudem adhuc et infirmum animum studiosi multitudine atque varietate rerum oneraverimus; duorum alterum, aut desertorem studiorum efficiemus, aut cum magno labore, sæpe etiam cum diffidentia, quæ plerumque juvenes avertit, serius ad id perducemus, ad quod, leviore via ductus, sine magno labore, et sine ulla diffidentia, maturius perduci potuisset.* I. I. I. 2.

[2] *Prima legum cunabula. In quatuor libros easdem Institutiones partiri jussimus, ut sint totius legitimæ scientiæ prima elementa.* Proem. § 3, 4.

But besides a regular Analysis of the Civil Law, which constitutes the main design of the ensuing work, there is a second, which is subsidiary to it, and may perhaps by some be thought the most useful as well as interesting of the two, namely, the comparison, which is, occasionally, made between the Roman Laws and those of England. Something of this sort was undertaken in the last century by the learned Dr Cowell, Professor of the Civil Law in the University of Cambridge, in a Latin work, entitled *Institutiones Juris Anglicani*, expressly composed and digested after the method and series of the Imperial Institutions. But besides that a scheme so forced and unnatural as that of reducing, throughout, the municipal laws of any one country to the model of those of any other, could not but be in its original extremely defective, much of the work here mentioned is now rendered useless, and to a common reader unintelligible, by the abolition of the Feudal Tenures, with an account and explanation of which a considerable portion of Dr Cowell's volume abounds: I could not therefore reap the fruit I expected and hoped for from this performance. The comparison I have aimed at is of a very different nature; and was made to serve the following, among other, important purposes: first, to point out any remarkable agreement or disagreement between the two systems, as often as either of these happened to occur: secondly, to shew in how many instances the English Law is plainly built on and borrowed from the Roman: and thirdly, to teach the younger part of my hearers how much that limited authority, delegated by our laws to the first magistrate of a free people, is to be preferred to the uncontrollable power usurped and exercised by a lawless despot[1]; from whence they may be able to form a

[1] Lord Lyttelton, in his useful History of Henry II. relates a curious anecdote from Giannoni (l. xii. c. 1.) with respect to the doctrine of the Imperial Law, on this point of absolute power, which it may not be without its use to transcribe. "The Emperor Frederic, surnamed Barbarossa, greatly favoured the professors of the Civil Law, and consulted them in the most important deliberations. Unhappily for him, one of these doctors, named Martin, maintained a thesis at Roncaglia against another, named Bulgarius, in which he asserted, that the Roman Emperor was, by right, the absolute master of the whole world, and of all the goods of particulars, so that he might dispose of them at his pleasure. This most abominable doctrine he drew from some parts of the Imperial Laws, and particularly from some words of Ulpian ill understood. But though his adversary, who was professor of the Civil Law at Pisa, endeavoured to vindicate that law from the imputation of so destructive a principle, the flattering doctor prevailed: his opinion was confirmed by a majority of professors, and Bartolus, one of the most celebrated commentators on the books of Justinian, declares it to be a *heresy* to contradict or deny it. In consequence of this judgment, Frederic set up such claims of despotic authority, as to raise in the Lombards, and other people of the empire, such an alarm for their liberties, as proved very troublesome and dangerous to him." Lyttelton, Book II. p. 206. vol. III. 8vo. ed. But notwithstanding the opinion of Bartolus, so dogmatically advanced, I own that for myself I am strongly inclined to favour the Bulgarian heresy: in confirmation of which, the following passages from the *Corpus Juris Civilis* may

just idea of the pre-eminence and superiority of our own constitution to that of imperial Rome. And here it becomes me to acknowledge the great

may be consulted. In the Digests (D. 32. l. 23.) we have this response of the lawyer Paulus. *Ex* imperfecto *testamento legata vel fidei-commissa* Imperatorem *vindicare,* inverecundum *est:* decet *enim tantæ majestati eas* servare *leges, quibus ipse* solutus *esse videtur.* Which is more fully explained in a constitution of the Emperor Alexander. (C. 6. 23. 3.) *Ex* imperfecto *testamento nec* Imperatorem *hæreditatem vindicare* posse, *sæpe constitutum est: licet enim lex imperii* solennibus juris *Imperatorem* solverit; *nihil tamen tam proprium imperii est, quam* legibus vivere. To the same purpose is a law of the Emperors Theodosius and Valentinian. (C. 1. 14. 4.) *Digna vox est majestate Regnantis,* legibus alligatum *se Principem profiteri: adeo de auctoritate juris nostra pendet auctoritas; et revera majus imperio est, submittere* legibus *principatum.* And Justinian himself, though in one of his Novels (Nov. cv.) he asserts, that *Deus ipsas* leges Imperatori *subjecit,* legem animatam *eum mittens hominibus;* yet in another place (I. 2. 17. 8.) affirms, as Severus and Antoninus had done before him, *Licet legibus* soluti simus, *attamen legibus* vivimus. Hence it should seem, that when it is said of an absolute prince that he is *solutus legibus,* the expression must be interpreted of such laws only as are *purely civil;* as, for instance, that seven witnesses should be necessary to make a *perfect* testament: and yet even to these, we find, it was always thought the prudent and decent part for him to conform, in order to set an example of obedience to his subjects. So that, after all that has been written on the famous text of Ulpian,* on which Martin chiefly supported his position, the words in effect amount to *little more* than a common maxim of the law of England, that the king, in his political capacity, can do no wrong. See the Treatise of Arthur Duck, *de Usu et Authoritate Juris Civilis Romanorum,* Lib. I. cap. 3. sect. xi. xii. with the authors he has quoted in the margin.

Claudian, in his Panegyric on the fourth consulship of Honorius, admirably describes the duty of a sovereign towards his people,

* *Princeps legibus solutus est* D. 1. 3. 31.

assistance I have received from the Commentaries on the Laws of England by the elegant author mentioned above; without which, I freely confess, I should not have executed this part of my work with half the advantage I have now been enabled to give it, when aided by his learned volumes. On this occasion, too, I will not neglect to own, that some help has been afforded me from the notes inserted by Dr Harris in his useful edition of Justinian's Institutions, which he has published in their original language, together with an English translation.

In a few cases I have remarked what seemed worthy of notice in the Roman Canon Law: some parts of which are very necessary to be adverted to by an English lawyer; especially the manner of computing the degrees of consanguinity by that law, without a knowledge of which no one can understand the doctrine of descents, or the mode of intestate succession to an estate in lands, as settled by the regulations of our own country. And indeed it may be observed with truth of that whole system,

people, in the following fine lines: which I will here subjoin, by way of relieving the tediousness of this long note.

> *In commune jubes si quid, censesve tenendum,*
> *Primus jussa subi: tunc observantior æqui*
> *Fit populus; nec ferre negat, cum viderit ipsum*
> *Auctorem parere sibi. Componitur orbis*
> *Regis ad exemplum: nec sic inflectere sensus*
> *Humanos* edicta *valent, ac* vita regentis.
>
> *De 4to Consulatu Honorii.* v. 295 *et seq.*

that however censurable it may be, when considered as calculated to support an unbounded supremacy in the Pope and Clergy, yet in another view, as a collection of rules and principles respecting the administration of justice, and the rights and properties of individuals, it merits no small share of praise; and, in conjunction with the Civil Law, certainly contributed to introduce more just and liberal ideas than had yet obtained of the nature of government, and the peace and order of society[1].

The author of the Commentaries speaking, in his introduction, of the study of the law, after having observed that a general acquaintance with the Roman jurisprudence has ever been deservedly regarded, even in England, as no small accomplishment of a gentleman, goes on to remark as follows: "Far be it from me to derogate from the study of the Civil Law, considered (apart from any binding authority) as a collection of written reason: no man is more thoroughly persuaded of the general excellence of its rules, and the usual equity of its decisions; nor is better convinced of its use as well as ornament to the scholar, the divine, the statesman, and even the common lawyer[2]." These words are so pertinent in themselves, and correspond so exactly to my own ideas of the worth and importance

[1] See the History of Charles v. by Dr Robertson, Vol. I. § 1. Art. vi.

[2] Introduction, § 1.

of the system I am here to explain, that in what remains of this preface, I shall content myself with enlarging on this *text*, and endeavouring to elucidate the truth and importance of the several particulars contained in it. In doing this, I wish not to exalt the Civil Law above its just measure: every liberal art has a natural connection, more or less remote, with every other; and every true friend of learning, far from making or insinuating invidious and often ill-founded comparisons, will labour to promote a friendly coalition between them all. The simple purpose I aim at is no more than this, to raise the profession, of which it is my lot to be appointed guardian, to that proper degree of credit, below which I am of opinion it has been unduly depressed; and to prove that it has at least as near an alliance with all the branches of polite literature, as any other that may be found in the whole family of sciences.

1. And first, with regard to the utility of the Roman Law to the Scholar, it needs but few words to shew, that a science so conversant as this in the great principles of justice and equity, which distinguishes with such care the boundaries of right and wrong, which teaches us the several relations we stand in to our fellow-creatures, and the rules by which our own conduct must be regulated, which is founded in human nature and applies to all the affairs of human life, between nation and nation,

man and man; must surely be entitled to one of the highest places in our esteem. It will be to entertain a very mean and disparaging opinion of the venerable monuments of ancient wisdom contained in the body of the Roman Law, to regard the rules there laid down for the decision of controverted points, whether of a public or private nature, as the maxims of mere lawyers: those great masters of legislation were as eminent for their skill in moral as in legal knowledge, and the sublimest notions both in philosophy and religion are inculcated in their writings. Accordingly we find them frequently called, among their other titles, *Juris Divini et Humani periti;* and the very definition of jurisprudence, given by Ulpian[1], like that of *Sapientia* by Cicero[2], is *Divinarum atque Humanarum rerum notitia.* This affinity between the study of law and philosophy has impressed a remarkably scientifical cast on the responses of the Roman Sages; and a competent knowledge of their tenets and principles is absolutely necessary in order to understand, with exactness and taste, the allusions to Roman customs and manners, which abound in the classical Latin authors, whether poets or historians. To which must be added, what will still more recommend this science to the polite scholar, the purity of the language, in which the pandects

[1] D. 1. 1. 10, 2. I. 1. 1. 1.

[2] Cic. de Offic. I. 43. and II. 2.

in particular are composed; which are held to be so perfect and elegant in point of style, that the Latin tongue might be retrieved from them, were all other Latin authors lost.

If the study of the Civil Law be thus useful to the Scholar in general, it must be still more eminently serviceable to the Academic in particular. It is admirably calculated to furnish the minds of youth with universal and leading notions, relating to natural and positive, to written and unwritten law: it instructs them in the various rights of persons, whether in a natural or civil capacity; the origin and rights of property; the grounds and reasons of testamentary and legal succession; the obligations arising from proper and improper contracts; the several species of civil injuries and crimes; together with the means of applying for and obtaining redress, and of bringing the guilty to condign punishment. These are matters of the utmost importance in themselves, peculiarly useful when considered as subjects of academical discipline, and no where more successfully illustrated than in the Cæsarean Law. Then, as said before, that it is written in a learned language, and bears an intimate relation with the Roman history and antiquities, are circumstances which recommend this science in a particular manner to young students; as they serve to place it in a middle way between the classical erudition they have gained at school, and the laws of their own country, to the study of which it is the best preparation. It was probably for some such reasons as these, that the Civil Law was made one of the three professions we are supposed to follow, in both our English Universities[1]; and both in this place and at Oxford, the profits of several fellowships are appropriated to the encouragement of it. A valuable privilege is likewise indulged to graduates in this faculty, by the Statute Law of the kingdom; Doctors and Bachelors of Laws, who have performed the customary exercises in order to such degrees, being permitted (by 21 Henry VIII. c. 13.) to hold two benefices with cure; which no Master of Arts can do without a chaplainship to some of the Royal Family, or to some Lord, or other person there mentioned, who is entitled to have chaplains. In the Universities also on the continent, where the connection between the Imperial and Municipal Laws is much more visible than in England, this art is taught, and considered as an almost necessary accomplishment of every gentleman: and in our associate kingdom of Scotland, where the Roman Law is of much more authority than with us, it is difficult, as Mr Justice Blackstone observes[2], to meet with a person of liberal education, who is destitute of a complete knowledge in that science, which is to be the

[1] See Appendix, No. I.

[2] Introduction to the Commentaries on the Laws of England, § 1.

guardian of his natural rights, and the rule of his civil conduct. The same author laments, in pathetic terms, the fashion, that has prevailed of late, for men of birth and distinction to send the growing hopes of their families to foreign academies, in order to attend lectures, conveyed in a dead or unknown language, on the Civil Law; where they are left at large, in a dangerous season of life, their morals and their studies both trusted to their own direction; and where, it is to be feared, they often imbibe opinions in religion and government, neither sort compatible with the generous spirit of civil and religious liberty, as professed in Britain. The only laudable way of removing so disgraceful a necessity, is to introduce a regular course of lectures on the Imperial Law at home; and at the same time so to contrive those lectures, as to prevent the danger, which might otherwise be apprehended, of instilling false or arbitrary principles into the mind, by laying hold of every proper opportunity of pointing out the defects of the Roman system, and the superior excellence of our own. But a design of this sort can no where be so successfully undertaken as at the Universities; where degrees in the faculty are actually conferred, and where a number of young gentlemen are collected from all parts of the kingdom, with the professed intention of being instructed how best to attain, what is surely the most important of human acquisitions, the knowledge of useful learning and of pure religion. How far in the following Analysis I have accomplished such a design, is not for me to say: but this I am bold to assert, that I have laboured faithfully to discharge the office committed to my care; and in whatever degree I may be thought to have fulfilled so weighty a trust, I have the conscious satisfaction of endeavouring at least, according to my measure, and to the best of my abilities, to contribute to the general good.

Besides the reasons now alledged, which evince the propriety of the study of the Civil Law, considered as a branch of academical education, there is another, which brings the matter still nearer to ourselves, namely, that it is the very law by which the two Universities of England are governed, and by which all civil controversies, excepting pleas of frank tenement, are directed to be decided. In the University of Cambridge in particular, the Statutes of Queen Elizabeth, given in the year 1570, and the decrees of the Senate, which are the established rules by which our academical behaviour is regulated, are unintelligible in those places where they treat of judicial proceedings, and of the method of prosecuting appeals, without a previous acquaintance with the ***Form of Private Judgments***, as settled in the Imperial Law[1]. And were some of those, who

[1] See Appendix, No. III. IV. V. which compare with Chap. IX. X. XI. of the Third Book of the Analysis; where the technical terms, in those numbers of the Appendix, are explained.

allow themselves to declaim on the inutility and unprofitableness of this science, to be asked to explain the meaning of certain parts of the statutes of their own Colleges, it is probable they would be not a little distressed how to return an answer, which might serve to conceal their ignorance, or justify their pretence to superior knowledge[1]. My reader will excuse me, if here I make a distinction: it is one thing to have a clear and luminous view of a subject throughout, which is the property of the true scholar only; and it is another thing to be barely capable of rendering into English a Latin word, which is the utmost perfection of knowledge in modern sciolists, and that too derived from no purer source than the muddy current of a dictionary.

2. It may perhaps seem strange to assert the utility of the Roman Law to the Divine. But when it is recollected that frequent allusions to this

[1] A story is told of Servius Sulpitius, when he consulted the famous Mutius Scævola on a point of law, which may be worth reciting. *Servius, cum in causis orandis primum locum, aut pro certo post M. Tullium obtineret, traditur ad consulendum Quintum Mucium de re amici sui pervenisse: cumque eum sibi respondisse de jure Servius parum intellexisset, iterum Quintum interrogasse; et a Quinto Mucio responsum esse, nec tamen percepisse; et ita objurgatum esse a Quinto Mucio; namque eum dixisse,* Turpe esse Patricio, et Nobili, et causas oranti, jus, in quo versaretur, ignorare. *Ea velut contumelia Servius tractatus, operam dedit Juri Civili: et—hujus volumina complura extant; reliquit autem prope centum et octoginta libros.* D. 1. 2. 2, 43.

law, in the instances of adoption, the right of citizenship, slavery, &c. occur in the New Testament, and especially in the writings of St Paul[2]; when it is remembered too that many of this profession are often called to preside as judges in the Spiritual Courts; and when it is further considered, how great a proportion the Civil Law bears in composing the Ecclesiastical Law of England; it will appear, that a competent skill in Roman jurisprudence is far from being foreign to the character of a Divine; as it qualifies him to understand with accuracy the original records of his faith, to support the dignity of his character as a spiritual judge, and to defend and secure the possession of his legal dues.

3. Nor will this study be less serviceable to the Statesman than to the Divine. It is impossible that foreign nations should carry on their transactions with each other without having recourse to some common standard, by which to regulate their disputes; and this common standard, by the consent of all, is the Roman Civil Law: in which

[2] See the Annotations of Grotius on the New Testament, particularly on the Acts of the Apostles, and the Epistles of St Paul; which are full of quotations from the Civil Law. This observation may be extended to another learned work of the same author, *De Jure Belli et Pacis;* which has a perpetual reference throughout to the Roman Customs and Laws, and cannot well be understood by one, who is destitute of all knowledge in this part of learning.

the rights and privileges of ambassadors, the interpretation of leagues and treaties, the incidents of war and peace, are discussed with a care and precision, in vain to be sought for in the institutions of other kingdoms. Those gentlemen therefore, who, on account of their birth or fortune, have the honour to be selected to personate their sovereign in foreign courts, would surely do well to acquaint themselves betimes with this great medium of national intercourse; that they may not be liable to be imposed on in their negotiations with statesmen of other kingdoms, but be qualified at the same time to do honour to themselves, and service to their country.

4. It remains, in the last place, that we shew the benefit which the Civil Law is able to afford even to the common lawyer. And here, though it be granted, that less of the Roman jurisprudence hath been introduced among us, than in any other country of Europe, and those, who apply to the study of the Common Law, often boast, and sometimes gratuitously enough, of this distinction; yet that certain parts and principles of the Imperial Law have been incorporated into our own, is a fact too incontestible to be denied. The learned Selden, in his Dissertation on Fleta[1] (a commentary on the English Law so called, because written by an unknown author, who was a prisoner in the *Fleet*, in

[1] Cap. 4.

the reigns of Edward II. and III.) has shewn, that during the greatest part of the subjection of this island to the Romans, or from the time of Claudius to that of Honorius, about 360 years, it was chiefly governed by the Cæsarean Law; within which interval, Papinian, Ulpian, Paulus, and others of the Roman lawyers, whose responses make so distinguishing a figure in the Pandects, presided in the seat of judgment in this kingdom. From the age of Honorius, the Saxon, Danish, and Norman customs took place, and continued for 740 years, without any intermixture, as is supposed, of the Imperial Law. But the fortunate discovery of the Pandects of Justinian, which was made in the middle of the 12th century by the Pisan soldiers at Amalfi, gave a new spirit to the study of this art, then sunk by means of the irruptions of the barbarous nations into an almost total oblivion, in Italy first, and afterwards in every other part of Europe. Lectures in the science were publicly read in England, by the famous Vacarius, under the patronage of Archbishop Theobald, both in the archiepiscopal palace at Lambeth, and at the University of Oxford; not long after Irnerius had opened a college for the same purpose at Bologna. And although the ardour of this new pursuit might in some measure be repressed by Stephen the then king, who, to gratify his own resentments against the Pope, had by an edict prohibited the teaching of the Roman Law; it was still studied with avidity in the schools and monasteries of the ecclesiastics, whose chief and favourite employment it was; and from the reign of Stephen to that of Edward III. that is, for the space of near 200 years, was held in great and general estimation[1].

And now, who will wonder that, with these advantages, the Civil Law should insinuate itself by insensible degrees into the system of English jurisprudence, and that the most venerable of our lawyers should not scruple to adopt the rules and reasonings of it, not only occasionally in the course of their pleadings, but more deliberately in their gravest and most serious compositions? The oldest publication on the Common Law now extant is that of Glanvil, Lord Chief Justice in the reign of Henry II. and the beginning of the Preface to that work is a direct imitation of the Proemium to the Institutions of Justinian. Both the words and the doctrine of the same book are quoted by Bracton, a judge in the time of Henry III. in his treatise *De Legibus ac Consuetudinibus Angliæ*, and he perpetually uses the Roman names of Titius and Sempronius, instead of the A and B of an English lawyer. Other authors, of name and credit,

[1] See the first of the two Dialogues of Dr Hurd, *On the Constitution of the English Government;* where the fate and fortunes of the Civil Law in England are delineated at large, with the usual elegance of this most learned Author.

have not scrupled, as occasion served, to use the maxims and rules of the Civil Law: and, as Wood observes[1], Fleta and Britton, and the most ancient of our writers, would look very naked, if every Roman lawyer should pluck away his feathers.

But we are not without other more direct proofs of the actual reception of the Roman Laws in Britain. The ingenious author of *Observations on the more ancient Statutes*[2] hath shewn, from several instances, that many ideas of our law have been plainly borrowed from the Roman. One of these instances is the power of the Attorney-General to file informations *ex officio;* which seems to be taken from the Civil Law, where there is always a public prosecutor. The denying of a felon to make his defence by an advocate, and not permitting his witnesses to be examined upon oath till the late Statute, are other examples of the like nature. To these we may add the form of trial in the Court of Chancery, evidently derived from the same source: here the complaint is by petition or bill, which answers to a libel; the defendant makes an answer in writing, which contains also his defence; to this succeed replications, exceptions, interrogatories, witnesses privately examined, a sentence of the judge in writing without the intervention of a jury: and, if necessary, an appeal also in writing to the Upper

[1] Preface to his Institute of the Imperial Law.

[2] Page 76. Edition 2d.

House of Parliament: and almost all the Chancellors or Judges of this Court, from Becket to Wolsey, that is, from the age next after the Conquest to the Reformation, were ecclesiastics and civilians. In testamentary causes, where our own laws are silent, or not sufficiently express, the Courts in England, which have cognizance of the distribution of the effects of persons dying intestate, are chiefly guided by the doctrine of one of Justinian's Novels. And, to mention no more, the Imperial Law, to this day, obtains, under different restrictions, in the Courts of Bishops and their officers, the Courts Military, the Courts of Admiralty, and the Courts of the two Universities: in all which it hath been received either by the consent of Parliament, and so is become a part of the Statute or Written Law; or by immemorial usage and custom, and thus constitutes an inferior branch of the Common or Unwritten Law. Every one, therefore, who would excel in his profession, either as a civilian or a common lawyer, ought to acquaint himself with the nature and jurisdiction of these several courts; in order to know exactly when they confine themselves within their proper limits; and when, in case of encroachment, they are liable to be restrained by prohibition.

Still it is not to be dissembled, that frequent instances occur in our history of great opposition made to the Civil Laws of Rome, whenever either the Crown or the Church have attempted, for reasons of their own, to introduce them into England. Nor is this circumstance, fairly estimated, any just objection to the real excellence of the laws themselves: for though, on the one hand, it were a mark of strange obstinacy or ignorance to deny, that the laws of England have received great improvements, by ingraftments from the Roman; yet, on the other hand, it ought also to be confessed, it was a wise caution of the barons to prevent these foreign laws from acquiring too great an authority; particularly in matters of that high nature, relating to government and the liberty of the subject. Again, it must be owned, that many of the Roman usages, such as slavery, adoption, the power of a father, substitutions, possession of goods, stipulations, and the like, are entirely unknown with us, and some of them abhorrent from the free and liberal spirit of our constitution. But, with all these deductions, it may still be maintained with truth, that the Civil Law is well deserving of the praises, which the learned of all countries have bestowed upon it, on account of its own inherent perfections. Nor have I the smallest scruple to assert, that the student, who confines himself to the institutions of his own country, without joining to them any acquaintance with those of Imperial Rome, will never arrive at any considerable skill in the grounds and theory of his profession: though he may perhaps attain to a certain mechanical readiness in the forms and practical parts of the law, he will not be able to comprehend that enlarged and general idea of it, by which it is connected with the great system of universal jurisprudence; by the knowledge of which alone he will be qualified to become a master in this art, and capable of applying it, as an honourable means of subsistence for himself, and of credit to his country[1].

Before I conclude, I beg leave to intreat the candour of those of my readers, whose superior abilities may enable them to discover any material errors in the following Analysis; and to assure them, that whatever mistakes are pointed out to me, they shall be rectified with thanks, in a future edition. Nor ought I to omit the opportunity, now afforded me, of expressing my grateful acknowledgments for the many instances of encouragement received from those, whose approbation I am most ambitious to procure; and for the attendance, with which my lectures have been honoured by persons of the highest rank and fortunes in the University.

[1] So at least the excellent author of the Commentaries, so often quoted in this Preface, seems to have thought; when he recommends it to the student, in order to qualify himself to enter on the study of the English Laws with advantage and reputation, first of all to impress on his mind the sound maxims of the law of nature, the best and most authentic foundation of human laws, and then to contemplate those maxims reduced to a practical system in the laws of Imperial Rome. Introduction, § 1.

I have no intentions, at present, to obtrude myself on the public by any further attempts to illustrate the Civil Law: the plan, which I had formed on my first entrance on this subject, is at length completed: it now remains that I return to those more serious and important studies, to which I had originally devoted myself and ministry, and from which (for I know not what should hinder me from confessing it) I should never have diverted, but from *profession* rather than *inclination*.

In the *second* edition of this Analysis I prefixed to each chapter a list of the books, by consulting which the several propositions may be explained. In this *third* edition many corrections with some additions are interspersed, which I hope may contribute to the greater perfection of the whole.

19 JANUARY, 1779.

ADVERTISEMENT

TO THE FOURTH EDITION.

THE Editor of the Fourth Edition acknowledges his obligation to the Professor of the Civil Law* for some additional references prefixed to several of the chapters, for some corrections of the text, and for a few notes which are distinguished from the notes of the author by being printed in the Italic character.

OCTOBER, 1795.

---

* The Rev. JOSEPH JOWETT, LL.D.

AN

ANALYSIS

OF

THE CIVIL LAW.

CONTENTS.

BOOK I.

THE RIGHTS OF PERSONS.

BOOK II.

THE RIGHTS OF THINGS.

BOOK III.

ACTIONS.

ROMAN CIVIL LAW.

BOOK I.

OF THE RIGHTS OF PERSONS.

CHAPTER I.

OF THE ROMAN CIVIL AND CANON LAWS, AND THEIR AUTHORITY IN ENGLAND.

Dig. Lib. I. Tit. 2. pr. § 1—14.
Duck *de Usu et Authoritate Juris Civilis Romanorum.*
Hoppii *Comment. ad Institutiones Justinianeas.* Præcognita Juris.
Heineccii *Antiquitates Romanæ.* Proemium.
——— *Elementa Juris Civilis.* Proemium.
Savigny's *History of the Roman Law.*
Taylor's *Elements of the Civil Law.* Introduction.
Bever's *Legal Polity of the Roman State.*
Burn's *Ecclesiastical Law.* Preface.
Dr Hurd's first Dialogue *On the Constitution of the English Government.*
Niebuhr's *History of Rome.*

1. THE systems of Roman Civil Law, before the age of the Emperor Justinian, were chiefly these. 1. Leges Regiæ; collected by Papirius. 2. Leges Decemvirales, or the Laws of the Twelve Tables. 3. *Jus Civile* Flavianum; to which the *Jus Civile* Ælianum was a Supplement. 4. Edictum Perpetuum Juliani. 5. The Codes of Gregory, Hermogenes and Theodosius.

2. The Imperial or Civil Law, as reformed by Justinian, consists of four parts. 1. The Institutions. 2. The Digests or Pandects. 3. The Code. 4. The Novels[1].

3. The Ecclesiastical or Canon Law is chiefly comprised, 1. in the Decree; 2. in the Decretals. The Decree has three parts; namely, (1) Distinctions; (2) Causes; (3) a Treatise concerning Consecration. The Decretals also are in three parts; namely, (1) Gregory's Decretals in five books; (2) the sixth Decretal; (3) the Clementine Constitutions.

[1] It may not be amiss, for the sake of beginners, to explain here the method of *quoting* the several parts, which now compose the Corpus Juris Romano-Civilis. The Institutions are contained in four books: each book is divided into titles; and each title into paragraphs; of which the first, described by the letters *pr.* or *princip.* is not numbered. The Digests or Pandects are in fifty books: each book is distributed into titles; each title into laws; and, very frequently, laws into paragraphs, of which the first is not numbered. The Code is comprised in twelve books; each of which is divided, like the digests, into titles and laws; and, sometimes, laws into paragraphs. The Novels are distinguished by their number, chapter and paragraph.

The old way of quoting was much more troublesome, by only mentioning the number or initial words, of the paragraph or law, without expressing either the number of book or title. Thus § *si adversus* 12. *Inst. de Nuptiis* means the 12th paragraph of the title in the Institutions *de Nuptiis,* which paragraph begins with the words *si adversus;* and which a modern civilian would cite thus, I. 1. 10. 12. So *l.* 30. *D. de R. J.* signifies the 30th law of the title in the digests *de Regulis Juris:* according to the modern way, thus, D. 50. 17. 30. Again, *l.* 5. § 3. *ff. de Jurejur.* means the 3d paragraph of the 5th law of the title in the digests *de Jurejurando:* according to the modern way, thus, D. 12. 2. 5. 3. And here note, that the digests are sometimes referred to, as in the last instance, by a double *f;* and at other times by the Greek Π or π.

The Extravagants of John XXII. and other later Popes were added as Novel Constitutions to the rest[2].

[2] The method of quoting the Roman Canon Law is as follows. The Decree, as said above, consists of Three Parts; of which the first contains 101 distinctions, each distinction being subdivided into canons: thus 1 *dist. c.* 3. *Lex* (or 1 *d. Lex*) is the first distinction, and 3d canon, beginning with the word *Lex*. The second part of the decree contains thirty-six causes; each cause comprehending several questions, and each question several canons: thus 3. *qu.* 9. *c.* 2. *Caveant* is cause the 3d, question the 9th, and canon the 2d, beginning with *Caveant*. The third part of the decree contains five distinctions, and is quoted as the first part, with the addition of the words *de Consecratione;* thus *de Consecr. dist.* 2. *can. Quia corpus* (or *can. Quia corpus* 35. *dist.* 2. *d. Consecr.*) means the 2d distinction, and the 35th canon, of the treatise *de Consecratione,* which canon begins with *Quia corpus.*

The Decretals are in three parts; of which the first contains Gregory's Decretals in five books; each book being divided into titles, and each title into chapters: and these are cited by the name of the title, and the number of the chapter, with the addition of the word *Extra,* or the capital letter X: thus, *c.* 3. *Extra de Usuris;* is the 3d chapter of the title in Gregory's Decretals, which is inscribed *de Usuris;* which title, by looking into the index, is found to be the 19th of the 5th book. Thus also, *c. cum contingat* 36. X. *de Offic. et Pot. Jud. Del.* is the 36th chapter, beginning with *Cum contingat,* of the title, in Gregory's Decretals, which is inscribed *de Officio et Potestate Judicis Delegati;* and which, by consulting the Index, we find is the 29th title of the 1st book. The sixth Decretal, and the Clementine Constitutions, each consisting of five books, are quoted in the same manner as Gregory's Decretals; only, instead of *Extra* or X, there is subjoined *in sexto* or *in* 6. and *in Clementinis* or in *Clem.* according as either part is referred to: thus, *c. Si gratiose* 5. *de Rescript. in* 6. is the 5th chapter, beginning with *Si gratiose,* of the title *de Rescriptis,* in the 6th Decretal; the title so inscribed being the 3d of the 1st book: and *Clem.* 1. *de Sent. et Re Judic.* (or *de Sent. et R. J. ut calum-*

4. The Canon Law of England comprehends, besides the collections of the Roman pontiffs, Legatine and Provincial Constitutions; and so far as it was received here before the statute of 25 Henry VIII. c. 19. and is not repugnant to the common law, the statute law, and the law concerning the king's prerogative, is acknowledged to be in force by the authority of parliament.

5. The Canons made in England in 1603, and never confirmed in parliament, so far as they are agreeable to the ancient Canon Law, bind the laity; so far as they contain new regulations, are binding on the clergy only.

6. The fate and fortunes of the Civil Law in Europe, and particularly in England.

niis. in Clem.) (or *c. ut calumniis.* 1. *de Sent. et R. J. in Clem.*) is the 1st chapter of the Clementine Constitutions, under the title *de Sententiâ et Re Judicatâ;* which chapter begins with *Ut calumniis,* and belongs to the 11th title of the 2d book.

The Extravagants of John XXII. are contained in one book, divided into fourteen titles: thus, *Extravag. Ad Conditorem. Joh.* 22. *de V. S.* means the chapter, beginning with *Ad Conditorem,* of the Extravagants of John XXII.; title, *de Verborum Significationibus.* Lastly, the Extravagants of later popes are called *Communes;* being distributed in five books, and these again into titles and chapters: thus, *Extravag. Commun. c. Salvator. de Præbend.* is the chapter, beginning with *Salvator,* among the *Extravagant Communes;* title, *de Præbendis.*

CHAPTER II.

OF LAW IN GENERAL; AND OF THE DIVISIONS AND PARTS OF THE CIVIL AND ENGLISH LAWS.

Inst. Lib. I. Tit. 1, 2.
Dig. Lib. I. Tit. 2. § 15—end.
——— Tit. 3, 4.
Hoppii *Comm.* Lib. I. Tit. 1, 2.
Heinecc. *Antiq. Rom.* Lib. I. Tit. 1, 2.
——— *El. J. C.* Lib. I. Tit. 2.
Wood's *Institute of the Civil Law.* Introduction.
Taylor's *El. of the Civ. Law:* art. *Law and Right; Public and Private Law; Pontifical Law; Justice, Equity; Law of Nature, Law of Nations, Civil Law: Lex. Plebiscitum, Senatus-Consultum, Prætor's Edicts, Responsa Prudentum, Imperial Constitutions; Custom.*
Grotius *de Jure Belli et Pacis.* Lib. I. C. 1.
Rutherforth's *Institutes of Natural Law.* Vol. I. ch. 2.
Blackstone's *Commentaries on the Laws of England.* Introduction. Sect. 1, 2.

1. JUSTICE is a disposition of mind to render to every one his right. Rights are perfect or imperfect: from the idea of Right is produced that of Obligation.

2. Law is a rule of action, prescribed by authority.

3. All Law is Natural or Instituted. In what manner the Law of Nature, the Law of Nations, and Civil Law, are distinguished from each other by the Roman lawyers.

4. The Roman people, when assembled to make Laws, were divided three ways, into what were called Curiæ, Centuriæ, Tribus: these assemblies were denominated Comitia Curiata, Centuriata, Tributa.

5. The Roman Civil Laws are of two kinds, 1. Written. 2. Unwritten. The Written Law is either Public or Private.

6. Of the Written Law there are six parts. 1. Lex. 2. Plebiscitum. 3. Senatus-consultum. 4. Edicta Magistratuum. 5. Responsa Prudentum. 6. Placita Principum.

7. Lex is, what was enacted by the whole body of the Roman people, assembled at the *Comitia Curiata* or *Centuriata;* at the recommendation of one of the greater magistrates.

8. Plebiscitum is, what was enacted by the plebeians, assembled at the *Comitia Tributa;* at the recommendation of a plebeian officer, the tribune.

9. In passing a law or plebiscite among the Romans, the method was, after previously putting it in writing at home, 1. Communication of it to the senate. 2. Promulgation. 3. Recitation at the *comitia.* To this succeeded, in case of no intercession by one or more of the tribunes, 4. *Sortitio,* or determination by lot of the order of voting, among the centuries or tribes. 5. *Regatio.* 6. Voting for or against the law, *per tabellas.* 7. *Suffragiorum diremptio.* 8. Confirmation.

10. Senatus-Consultum is a decree of the senate, concerning such things as were committed to their jurisdiction; which had not properly the force of law, unless confirmed by the people.

11. The method of making a decree of the senate, during the times of the Roman Republic, was 1. Proposing it by one of the consuls, or the prætor; which was called *Relatio ad Senatum.* 2. *Rogatio.* 3. Voting for or against the decree, *per*

discessionem. 4. Putting the decree in writing. 5. Confirmation. After the destruction of the Republic, the decrees of the senate were little more than the will of the emperor, declared *mediante Senatu.*

12. Edicta Magistratuum are edicts of the prætors and ediles; which together made up the system, called *Jus Honorarium.*

13. Responsa Prudentum are opinions of those, to whom it was permitted to answer authoritatively on matters of law. These, collected together, were called, emphatically, *Jus Civile.*

14. Placita Principum are constitutions of the Roman emperors. These were, 1. General. 2. Special. The general were, (1) *Epistolæ;* (2) *Decreta;* (3) *Edicta.* The special were called *Privilegia.*

15. The Unwritten Law is Custom.

16. The Laws of England are also of two kinds. 1. The Written or Statute Law. 2. The Unwritten or Common Law.

17. The Ecclesiastical Law of England is composed of the Civil, Canon, Common and Statute Laws.

18. Equity is the correction of the Written Law, when, on account of its generality, it is too rigid or defective.

19. The Objects of the Civil Law are, I. The Rights of Persons. II. The Rights of Things. III. Actions, or the means of recovering by law what is due.

CHAPTER III.

OF PERSONS IN GENERAL; AND OF FREEMEN AND SLAVES.

Inst. Lib. I. Tit. 3—8.
Hoppii *Comm.* Lib. I. Tit. 3—8.
Heinecc. *A. R.* } Tit. 3—8.
———*El. J. C.* }
Wood's *Inst. of the Civ. Law.* Book I. ch. 1. 2.
Esprit des Loix. Liv. XV.
Lettres Persanes. Lett. 115.
Taylor's *El. of the Civ. Law.* art. *Persons* and *Servitude.*
Grotius *de J. B. et P.* Lib. II. C. V. § 27, 29, 30. C. XXII. § 11. Lib. III. C. VII.
Rutherforth's *Inst. of Nat. Law.* Vol. I. ch. 20.
Wood's *Institute of the Laws of England.* B. I. ch. 1.
Blackstone's *Comm.* B. I. ch. 14. B. II. ch. 6.
Sullivan's *Lectures on the Feudal and English Laws.* Lect. 24, 25.
Observations on the more ancient Statutes. Ed. 3, 1769.
Ld. Lyttelton's *Hist. of Henry II.* Book II.
Robertson's *Hist. of Charles V.* Vol. I. note ix.
Hargrave's *Arguments on the case of Sommerset, a Negro.* Lond. 1772.

1. PERSONS are considered either in their Natural or Civil capacities.

2. In their Natural capacity, they are considered with regard to, 1. Life. 2. Sex. 3. Age.

3. In their Civil capacity, their state is denominated from a respect to, 1. Liberty. 2. City. 3. Family.

4. The first division of persons, in a Civil consideration, is into Freemen and Slaves.

5. Slavery, in the Civil Law, had three origins. 1. Captivity in war. 2. Birth. 3. The sale of a man's self to another. None of these are justifiable causes of slavery.

6. Aristotle's opinion of natural slavery is groundless.

7. Slaves were 1. Ordinary. 2. Peculiar; otherwise called Vicarial.

8. The power of a master over his slave consisted in three things. 1. He could put him to death. 2. He could transfer him, by sale or gift, to whom he pleased. 3. Whatever the slave acquired belonged to his master.

9. This power was greatly abridged by the later emperors.

10. The decline of domestic slavery in Europe was greatly owing to the Christian religion. The baptism of heathen slaves makes no alteration in their civil condition.

11. Freemen were, 1. Ingenui. 2. Libertini.

12. The condition of the mother determined the state of her child, as to freedom or slavery.

13. The Law of England differed in this respect from the Civil Law.

14. A Libertinus was one, who from a slave became free by manumission. The rights of the former master to the services of such a person were called *Jura Patronatûs.*

15. By the ancient laws of Rome, liberty could only be conferred three ways. 1. *Censu.* 2. *Vindicta.* 3. *Testamento.*

16. Other less solemn ways of manumission were afterwards introduced by the Roman emperors.

17. The several ways of manumission did not all confer the same degree of freedom: but the *Libertini* were of three sorts. 1. *Cives Romani.*

2. *Latini sive Juniani.* 3. *Dedititii.* This distinction was abolished by Justinian.

18. The *Lex Ælia Sentia,* which restrained a master from manumitting his slaves in certain cases; and the *Lex Fusia Caninia,* intended to limit testamentary manumissions; and the alterations in these laws by Justinian; explained.

19. Villenage, as formerly known in England, was a state little better than slavery among the Romans. The subjects of this state, if males, were called Villeins; if females, Neifs. A villein was either *regardant* to a manor, or *in gross.*

20. Villeins might be enfranchised by manumission; which was, 1. Express. 2. Implied.

21. Copyhold tenures, now subsisting in England, are descended from the ancient Villenage.

22. Villenage, though never *formally* abolished by any statute, was at last, insensibly, forgotten.

23. The revival of domestic slavery in America affords no proof, that the introduction of a new slavery into England is now lawful.

24. Slavery is declared unlawful by 3 and 4 William IV. c. 73, from the 1st of August, 1834.

CHAPTER IV.

OF CITIZENS AND STRANGERS; NATIVES AND ALIENS; BY THE ROMAN AND ENGLISH LAWS.

Heinecc. *A. R.* Appendix Libri Primi.
Grandeur et Decadence des Romains. ch. 9.
Wood's *Inst. of the Civ. Law.* B. I. ch. 2.
Blackstone's *Comm.* B. I. ch. 10.

1. THE second division of persons, in a civil consideration, is into Citizens and Strangers. This division is wholly omitted by Justinian in his Institutions.

2. The persons subject to the Roman government were classed under four denominations. They were, 1. Cives. 2. Latini. 3. Italici. 4. Provinciales. Those who neither belonged to the city of Rome, nor to any state subject to the Romans, were called Hostes and Peregrini.

3. No one could be a citizen of Rome and of any other city, at the same time.

4. By a constitution of the Emperor Antoninus Caracalla, the privileges of a Roman citizen were conferred on all the inhabitants of every part of the Roman empire, who were Ingenui: and the same privileges were afterwards extended, by Justinian, to the Libertini.

5. Of the states subject to the Roman empire, some were Municipia, others Præfecturæ, others Coloniæ.

6. Of Natives, Aliens, and Denizens, by the laws of England.

CHAPTER V.

OF THE POWER OF THE FATHER.

Inst. Lib. I. Tit. 9. 12.
Hoppii *Comm.* Lib. I. Tit. 9. 12.
Heinecc. *A. R.* } Lib. I. Tit. 9.
——— *El. J. C.* } 12.
Wood's *Inst. of the Civ. Law.* B. I. ch. 2.
Esprit des Loix. Liv. V. ch. 7. Liv. VII. ch. 10. 11.
Taylor's *El. of the Civ. Law.* art. *Power of the Father.*
Bynkershoek *de Jure occidendi liberos.*
Noodtii Julius Paulus.
Grotius *de J. B. et P.* Lib. II. ch. 5.
Wood's *Inst. of Laws of England.* B. I. ch. 6.
Blackstone's *Commen.* B. I. ch. 16.

1. THE third division of persons in their civil capacity, is into Patres-familias and Filios-familias.

2. The reciprocal duties of parents and children, by the Civil and English laws.

3. The power of a Roman father consisted in three things. 1. He could put his child to death; which power formed a domestic tribunal in each family. 2. He could sell him three times. 3. Whatever the son acquired belonged to his father.

4. The steps, by which this power was reduced by the Roman Emperors.

5. The natural death of the father, and the civil death of either father or son, put an end to the *Patria Potestas.*

6. If the father was taken captive, his power was suspended during his captivity, and on his return revived by what was called *Jus Postliminii.*

7. The father could put an end to his power by emancipation: the regulations made in this ceremony by Justinian.

CHAPTER VI.

OF MARRIAGE.

Inst. Lib. I. Tit. 10.
Hoppii *Comm.* Lib. I. Tit. 10.
Heinecc. *A. R.* } Lib. I. Tit. 10.
——— *El. J. C.* }
Wood's *Inst. of the Civ. Law.* B. I. ch. 2.
Esprit des Loix. Liv. XVI.
Taylor's *El. of the Civ. Law.* art. *Marriage.*
Huberi *prælectio ad Inst.* Lib. I. Tit. 10. § 10.
Et ad Dig. XXIII. ii. 5.

Novell. XXII.
Grot. *de J. B. et P.* Lib. II. ch. 5.
Rutherforth's *Inst. of Nat. Law.* Vol. I. ch. 15.
Wood's *Inst. of the Laws of England.* B. I. ch. 6.
Burn's *Eccl. Law.* Title, *Wills.*
Blackstone's *Comm.* B. I. ch. 15.
Nuptiæ Sacræ.

1. THE *Patria Potestas* was acquired three ways. 1. By lawful Marriage. 2. By Legitimation. 3. By Adoption.

2. Nuptiæ and Matrimonium were different. The Solennes Nuptiæ of the Romans were completed Farre, Coemptione, Usu: and might be dissolved Diffarreatione, Remancipatione, Usurpatione.

3. When the Marriage-Contract is said to be formed by consent alone, it was supposed to be such a consent, as excluded, not only error and fraud, but force and fear.

4. Impediments to a just Marriage, by the Roman Law, were, 1. Non-consent of the parent. (How far this consent is necessary by the law of England.) 2. Want of age. 3. Want of citizenship. 4. Natural defects of mind and body. 5. Consanguinity. 6. Affinity.

5. The Rules for computing Degrees of Consanguinity, in the Right and Oblique lines, by the Civil and Canon and English laws.

A
B
C D
E F
G H
I

6. General Rule concerning marriages prohibited on account of consanguinity and affinity; "All such as are *real* parents and children to each other, or *in the place* of parents and children, are forbidden to marry together."

7. In the Right line, marriages were prohibited *in infinitum;* whether the relation of parent or child were derived from nature, or introduced by adoption, and that dissolved.

8. In the Oblique line, marriages of brothers and sisters, of the whole blood or half, natural or adopted, whilst the adoption continued; as also of uncles and nieces, and of aunts and nephews, were forbidden: but from the time of the Emperor Claudius to that of Constantine, the marriage of a brother's daughter had been allowed.

9. The marriage of a great aunt, or the widow of a great uncle, though forbidden by the Roman, is allowed by the English laws.

10. The marriages of first cousins, which, at different times, had been both allowed and forbidden by the Emperors before Justinian, were by him declared to be lawful.

11. Marriages in the Right line were forbidden on account of affinity no less than consanguinity. In the Oblique line, the old Roman lawyers compared affinity with adoption, and made the same

rules govern both; but the constitutions of the Emperors forbad marriages of persons related by affinity in this line.

12. *Comprivigni*, or children by former marriages of a husband or wife, might marry together.

13. The prohibitions of marriage, on account of consanguinity and affinity, extended equally to freemen and slaves.

14. Laws concerning second marriages.

15. Impediments to a just-marriage, by the laws of England, are, 1. Canonical. 2. Civil. It is enacted by 5 and 6 William IV. c. 54. that *all* marriages which shall hereafter be celebrated between persons within the prohibited degrees of consanguinity or affinity, shall be absolutely null and void.

16. Effects of the marriage-contract are, 1. Common to husband and wife. 2. Peculiar to one only.

17. Polygamy was condemned by the Roman law, during the Republic, and by the constitutions of the Emperors: it is punished in England with transportation or imprisonment, according to 9 Geo. IV. c. 31.

18. Divorces were, 1. *Bona gratia.* 2. *Mala gratia.*

19. The tradition, that there was no instance of a divorce in Rome, till the year of the city 525, is at least a questionable piece of history.

20. In England, divorces are, 1. Total, *a vinculo matrimonii.* 2. Partial, *a mensa et thoro.*

CHAPTER VII.

OF LEGITIMATION.

Inst. Lib. I. Tit. 10. § 13.
Hoppii *Comm.* Lib. I. Tit. 10. § 13.
Heinecc. *A. R.* } L. I. Tit. 10.
——— *El. J. C.* } Appendix.
Wood's *Inst. of the Civ. Law.* B. I. ch. 2.

Burn's *Eccl. Law.* Title, *Bastards.*
Blackstone's *Comm.* B. I. ch. 16.
——— *Law Tracts. On the Great Charter.* Introduction, p. lxxxiii—lxxxviii. 8vo.

1. LEGITIMATE children were those born in lawful wedlock; all others were considered as Illegitimate.

2. Illegitimate children were of four sorts. 1. Natural children, or those born in concubinage. 2. Spurious. 3. *Filii Adulterini.* 4. *Incestuosi.* The first of these were the only objects of Legitimation.

3. Legitimation was procured three ways: 1. By a subsequent marriage. 2. By the natural son being made a decurion. 3. By rescript from the emperor.

4. Bastards, by the laws of England, are such children, as are born out of lawful wedlock: nor will the subsequent marriage of the parents legitimate such children, as it would by the Civil and Canon Laws.

5. Children born so long after the death of the husband, that, by the usual course of nature, they could not be begotten by him, are bastards. The

process in England *de ventre inspiciendo* is exactly agreeable to the rules of the Civil Law.

6. Children born during wedlock may, in some cases, be bastards.

7. Rights and incapacities of bastards: the different senses of the word *mulier*, in the English law.

CHAPTER VIII.

OF ADOPTION.

Inst. Lib. I. Tit. 11.	Heinecc. *A. R.* } Lib. I. Tit. 11.
Hoppii *Comm.* Lib. I. Tit. 11.	——— *El. J. C.* } Lib. I. Tit. 11.

1. ADOPTION was of two kinds, arrogation, and adoption, specifically so called: the ceremonies in both kinds explained.

2. Adoption *in specie* was, 1. *Plena.* 2. *Minus plena.*

3. He who arrogated or adopted a son was to be older than that son by eighteen years; in the case of a grandson, he was to be older by thirty-six years.

4. Effects of arrogation and adoption.

5. Adoption was never practised in England, nor have we any laws concerning it.

6. In Germany there is a sort of adoption, called *Unio seu parificatio prolium;* by which children by former marriages of husband and wife are made equal to one another, in regard to succession.

7. The Roman custom of adoption is frequently alluded to in the New Testament.

CHAPTER IX.

OF GUARDIANSHIP.

Inst. Lib. I. Tit. 13—26.
Hoppii *Comm.* Lib. I. Tit. 13—26.
Heinecc. *A. R.* } Lib. I. Tit.
——— *El. J. C.* } 13—26.
Wood's *Inst. of Civ. Law.* B. I. ch. 2.

Wood's *Inst. of the Laws of England.* B. I. ch. 6.
Burn's *Eccl. Law.* Title, *Wills.*
Blackstone's *Comm.* B. I. ch. 8. 17. B. II. ch. 5, 6. 19.
Fonblanque's *Equity.* B. II. 2. 2.

1. ANOTHER division of persons, derived from the last of parent and child, is that of guardian and ward. Guardianship was of two kinds. I. Tutela. II. Cura. The objects of the first kind are called pupils; of the second, minors. In England, the guardian performs the offices of both tutor and curator of the Roman laws.

2. In the Roman guardianship, some things were peculiar to each kind, taken separately; others belonged to both in common.

I.

3. Tutela was of three sorts. I. Testamentary. II. Legal. III. Dative.

4. I. In the testamentary tutelage, it was required, 1. That the person appointing should be a parent, who had the child under power. 2. The child was to be an *impubes.* 3. The appointment was to be by a last will.

5. There are four kinds of guardians in England. 1. By Common Law: who are, (1) By nature;

(2) For nurture; (3) In socage. 2. By Statute Law. 3. By particular custom. 4. By election. The guardian by Statute Law answers to the testamentary tutor of the Romans.

6. II. When there was no testamentary tutor *tàm re quàm spe*, the legal tutelage took place.

7. The *Tutor Legitimus*, by the Civil Law, was the nearest relation by the male side, to whom the inheritance, in case of intestacy, would descend. The name of such relation was *Agnatus*.

8. The legal guardian in England is the nearest relation, to whom the inheritance, in case of intestacy, does *not* descend.

9. Any such change in the condition of an *Agnatus* as destroyed the *agnatio*, at the same time destroyed the legal tutelage.

10. Such a change of state was called capitis diminutio; and was of three sorts. 1. *Maxima*. 2. *Media*. 3. *Minima*.

11. By a constitution of Justinian, the mother and grandmother were sometimes preferred to the tutelage, in exclusion of the *Agnati*.

12. A second species of the *Legitima Tutela* was that of the patron to his libertus: the patron was expressly called, by the Decemviral Law, to the succession of his *libertus*, dying intestate; and was therefore virtually called to the tutelage also.

13. A third species was that of a parent to his emancipated child: this was founded on the ancient ceremony of emancipation; by which the parent was considered as a *quasi-patronus*, and the child as his *quasi-libertus*.

14. A fourth species was that called Fiduciaria Tutela: this related to one under the age of puberty, who had been emancipated by a parent that was dead. The three examples are, 1. Of a father to his son, emancipated by the grandfather. 2. Of a brother to his emancipated brother. 3. Of the *patruus* to an emancipated nephew.

15. Women, by the Roman law, were under perpetual tutelage. This *Tutela Muliebris* devolved, like that of pupils, on the *Proximus Agnatus;* but might be transferred by him to the next in degree.

16. III. The dative tutelage was assigned by the magistrate. The *Lex Atilia*, and *Lex Julio-Titia* explained.

17. The regulations in the dative tutelage, made by the Emperors Claudius and Justinian.

18. The office of a tutor consisted in three things. 1. In taking care of the education of his pupil. 2. In administering his affairs. 3. In giving authority to the acts of the pupil. In England, the office of the guardian is all administration.

19. The tutor was not obliged to give up his accounts, till after the expiration of his office. A contrary practice now generally obtains in England.

20. A pupil, if very near the age of puberty, though he could not be under a *civil* obligation, might be under a *natural* one. In matters of crimes and offences, the rule, by the Civil and English laws, is, *Malitia supplet ætatem.*

21. In case of a suit between tutor and pupil, the prætor appointed another tutor, in whose name the suit was carried on: Justinian changed this

prætorian tutor into a curator, specially created for the purpose. The *prochein ami*, or next friend of the minor, in England, supplies the place of this curator, in the Civil Law.

22. The *Tutela* was ended, 1. On the part of the pupil; (1) by puberty; (2) by death, natural or civil; (3) by arrogation. 2. On the part of the tutor; (1) by death, natural or civil; (2) by the office of the magistrate; *volente Tutore, vel invito.*

II.

23. When the tutela was at an end, the Cura began. In England, he, who mostly resembles the Roman curator, is the guardian, whom a minor chooses for himself, after he is fourteen years of age.

24. Whether a curator could be given to a minor against his will, is a question among the Roman lawyers. History of curation from its beginning.

25. Lunatics, and prodigals, who were reckoned *quasi* lunatics, were put under the government of curators. In England, idiots and lunatics have tutors assigned them to protect their *persons*, and curators to manage their *estates:* but no notice is taken of prodigals, as in the Civil Law.

26. In some particular cases, pupils, as well as minors, were under the government of curators.

27. The *Cura* was ended, 1. on the part of the minor; (1) by his becoming a major; (2) by the *Venia Ætatis;* (3) by death, natural or civil; (4) by arrogation. 2. On the part of the curator; (1) by death, natural or civil; (2) by the office of the magistrate; *volente Curatore, vel invito.*

III.

28. Before either tutor or curator could exercise his office, he gave security for his fidelity, by what was called *Cautio Fide-jussoria.* When there were several tutors or curators, any one that offered the fidejussory caution had the acting part, in preference to the rest.

29. If the magistrate neglected to take sureties, or took such as were not good, he was liable to the *Actio Subsidiaria,* which extended to his heirs.

30. Excuses, by which tutors and curators were relieved from the burthen of guardianship, may be reduced to three heads. 1. *Ob Privilegium.* 2. *Impotentiam.* 3. *Existimationis periculum.* The laws of England are silent concerning the excuses of guardians, no one with us being compelled to take the office.

31. Tutors and curators were liable to be removed by the magistrate, *tanquam Suspecti.*

Guardians may be removed in England.

CHAPTER X.

OF CORPORATIONS.

Dig. Lib. III. Tit. 4.
Lib. XLVII. Tit. 22.
Wood's *Inst. of the Civ. Law.* B. I. ch. 2.
Taylor's *El. of the Civ. Law.* art. *S. C. Marcionum.* p. 567—573. 4to.
Wood's *Inst. of Laws of England.* B. I. ch. 8.
Blackstone's *Comm.* B. I. ch. 18.

1. BESIDES the former divisions of persons, considered in their natural and civil capacities; there are also artificial persons, called in the Civil Law Universitates, and Collegia; and in the laws of England, Bodies Politic, or Corporations.

2. Corporations were constituted by public authority. In England, they may subsist four ways. 1. By Common Law. 2. Prescription. 3. Letters Patent of the King. 4. Act of Parliament.

3. Three persons, at least, were required to constitute a corporation; though it could subsist, if the community were afterwards reduced to one. In England, corporations are sole or aggregate: and are further divided into, 1. Lay; which are, (1) Civil; (2) Eleemosynary. 2. Spiritual. 3. Mixt.

4. Corporations were possessed of various powers. 1. They had a common name, and seal. 2. They could sue or be sued by their common name. 3. Could borrow money by their *Syndic.* 4. Take lands, with special privilege from the Emperor. 5. Make laws for their own government called *Statutes,* and in

England *By-laws*, provided they were not contrary to the law of the land.

5. In corporations, the act of the major part was esteemed the act of all. In England, the act of any majority is esteemed the act of the whole body, notwithstanding the private statutes of any corporation to the contrary.

6. The visitatorial power is exercised to correct all irregularities that may arise in corporations, and to promote the observance of the statutes and regulations that have been prescribed.

7. A corporation, as such, could not commit offences or crimes; but delinquents, in their personal capacity, were answerable for any misbehaviour. The same practice obtains in England.

8. Corporations might be dissolved, 1. By forfeiture. 2. By the death of all their members. In England, a sole corporation can only be dissolved by surrender of its franchises to the King, or by Act of Parliament.

BOOK II.

OF THE RIGHTS OF THINGS.

CHAPTER I.

OF PROPERTY IN GENERAL.

Inst. Lib. II. Tit. 1. pr. § 1—10.
Hoppii *Comm.* Lib. II. Tit. 1. pr. § 1—10.
Heinecc. *A. R.* Lib. II. Tit. 1. § 1—20.
——— *El. J. C.* Lib. II. Tit. 1. § 310—339.
Wood's *Inst. of the Civ. Law.* B. II. ch. 1.
Taylor's *El. of the Civ. Law.* art. *Property.* p. 448—479.
Grotius *de J. B. et P.* Lib. II. C. II. III.
Rutherforth's *Inst. of Nat. Law.* vol. I. ch. 3. 5.
Blackstone's *Comm.* B. I. ch. 1. 2. 3. 24.
Vattel. *Droit des Gens.* B. 4. 7.
Zouch. *De Legati Delinquentis Judice.*

1. THE subjects of Property are called Res, things.

2. In things are to be considered, I. Their kinds. II. The rights, which may be acquired in them. III. The ways of acquiring those rights.

3. I. Things were, 1. *Extra patrimonium,* that is, incapable of being possessed by single persons, exclusively of others. 2. *In patrimonio,* that is, capable of being so possessed.

4. Things *Extra patrimonium* were of four sorts. 1. Things common. 2. Things public. 3. Things belonging to a society or corporation, called res universitatis. 4. Things consecrated to religious uses, called (1) *Res sacræ;* (2) *Religiosæ;* (3) *Sanctæ.*

5. Things *In patrimonio*, called res singulorum, were of two sorts. 1. Corporeal; which included, (1) Moveables; (2) Immoveables. 2. Incorporeal.

6. By the laws of England, things are distributed into two kinds. 1. Things real. 2. Things personal. Things real consist in 1. Lands. 2. Tenements. 3. Hereditaments; which last are, (1) Corporeal; (2) Incorporeal. Things personal are called chattels; which are (1) Chattels real; (2) Chattels personal.

7. II. The substance of things, in the earliest ages, belonged to mankind in common; yet even then, there was a temporary right to the use, which supplied the place of property.

8. The inconveniences of such a communion of goods occasioned, in time, the introduction of a permanent and exclusive right to the substance as well as use of things. This permanent and exclusive right is called property.

9. Property in things might be, 1. In possession. 2. In action. The former is called dominion, or *jus in re:* the latter, obligation, or *jus ad rem.* The same distinction obtains in England, with regard to property in things moveable or chattels personal.

10. Dominion in things is, 1. Simple, called *dominium plenum.* 2. Qualified, called *dominium minus plenum.* The latter is of two kinds. (1) *Directum.* (2) *Utile.*

11. Other divisions of *dominium* into *eminens et vulgare; quiritarium et bonitarium;* explained.

12. III. The ways of acquiring a right to things are derived, I. From the Law of Nature or Nations. II. From the Civil Law.

CHAPTER II.

OF THE NATURAL MODES OF ACQUIRING PROPERTY.

Inst. Lib. II. Tit. 1. § 11—47. Tit. 8.
Hoppii *Comm.* Lib. II. Tit. 1. § 11—47. Tit. 8.
Heinecc. *A. R.* Lib. I. Tit. 1. § 21—29. Tit. 8.
——— *El. J. C.* Lib. II. Tit. 1. § 340—348. Tit. 8.
Wood's *Inst. of the Civ. Law.* B. II. ch. 3.
Grotius *de J. B. et P.* Lib. II. C. III, VIII. X.
Wood's *Inst. of Laws of Eng.* B. II. ch. 3.
Blackstone's *Comm.* B. I. ch. 8. B. II. ch. 16. 19. 20. 21. 25. 26. 27.
Sullivan's *Lectures on the Feudal and English Laws.* Lect. 12. 15. 17.

1. THE natural modes of acquiring a right to things are three. I. Occupancy. II. Accession. III. Tradition.

2. I. Occupancy is the taking possession of such things as had been possessed by no one before, called res nullius.

3. Under the head of Occupancy are considered, 1. The right of property in animals. 2. Captures in war. 3. Things found.

4. The right of property in animals is different, according to their different kinds. Animals are of three sorts; *feræ, mansuetæ, mansuefactæ naturæ.*

5. The right of property in animals *feræ naturæ* may be restrained by positive laws. These restrictions may regard, 1. The place. 2. The persons. 3. The animals.

6. Occupancy in war extends both to the *goods* and *persons* of enemies. Captives taken in war, recovering their liberty, were reinstated in their ancient rights, by the fiction called *jus postliminii.*

7. Occupancy in things found, relate, 1. to such things as never had an owner: as precious stones, gems, &c. found on the *surface* of the earth or sea. 2. To things which cease to have an owner: as treasure trove and derelicts.

8. Treasure trove is treasure hidden *in* the earth or other secret place, the owner being unknown.

9. Derelicts are things wilfully abandoned by the owner, with an intention to leave them for ever. In England, there is no such thing as a derelict. Of waifs and estrays in the English laws.

10. Things lost by negligence, or chance, or thrown away upon necessity, are not derelicts. The *Lex Rhodia de Jactu*[1]; and the law of England concerning wrecks, and the goods called *jetsam, flotsam,* and *ligan,* explained.

11. Real property, by the law of England, cannot now be acquired by the title of *common* occupancy; although that of *special* occupancy still subsists: but this does not extend to such estates as are copyhold.

12. II. Accession is the right of acquiring the increase or improvements made in things that are our own: and is, 1. Natural. 2. Industrial. 3. Mixt.

13. Natural accessions are, 1. The brood of female slaves and cattle. 2. River increments or

[1] D. 14. 2.

alluvions. 3. Land acquired by the force of a river. 4. Islands rising in the sea, or in a public river. 5. Channels deserted by a river.

14. The Roman laws concerning natural accessions have been generally adopted by the laws of England: but in the case of an island rising in the sea, where the Civil Law gives it to the first occupant, the English law gives it to the king.

15. Industrial accessions are, 1. Specification, or producing a new form from another's materials. 2. Conjunction, where two things are joined together, their substances remaining distinct and separate. 3. Confusion, or the mixture of liquids. 4. Commixtion, or the mixture of solids. 5. Building; (1) on a man's own ground, with another's materials; (2) On another's ground, with his own materials. 6. Writing. 7. Painting.

16. Mixt accessions are, 1. Planting. 2. Sowing. 3. The fruits gathered, and consumed, by the *bonâ fide* possessor of another's property.

17. The doctrine of the Roman and English laws on industrial and mixt accessions; and the opinion of Grotius on this subject; examined.

18. III. By the old Roman laws, alienation of things corporeal was of two kinds. 1. Mancipation. 2. Tradition. The former related to such things as were called *res mancipi;* the latter to the *res nec mancipi.* Justinian abolished the distinction; and gave to tradition, or simple delivery, all the effects of the ancient mancipation.

19. No tradition was good, unless, 1. preceded by a sufficient cause of *consideration.* 2. Made by one who had a right to alienate. It might happen

in some cases, that the real owner could not alienate; and he, who was not the owner, could.

20. Tradition was three-fold. 1. True. 2. Feigned; which was, (1) *Brevi manu.* (2) *Longa manu.* 3. Symbolical.

21. Ways of alienation of real property, in England, by deed, feoffment with livery of sezin, lease, and release; explained.

CHAPTER III.

OF RIGHTS OR THINGS INCORPOREAL; AND OF REAL AND PERSONAL SERVICES.

Inst. Lib. II. Tit. 2—5.
Hoppii *Comm.* Lib. II. Tit. 2—5.
Heinecc. *A. R* } Lib. II. Tit.
——— *El. J. C.* } 2—5.
Wood's *Inst of the Civ. Law.* B. II. ch. 2.
Rutherforth's *Inst. of Nat. Law.* vol. I. ch. 4.
Blackstone's *Comm.* B. II. ch. 3. art. IV. and ch. 8.

1. RIGHTS in things are incorporeal, and capable only of an improper or *quasi*-possession; which is proved from the allowed use and exercise of those rights.

2. Services are rights, which one person has in the land or building of another; by which the owner is limited in the use of his property, and obliged either to *suffer*, or *not to do* something in his own land or building, for the benefit of another person, who has a claim upon it.

3. Services are of two kinds. 1. Real (which are sometimes called predial). II. Personal.

4. I. Real services are rights, which one estate owes to another estate: these are, 1. Rural. 2. City services.

5. Rural services are those belonging to lands, and are all affirmative. City services are those, which belong to buildings for the habitation of men; and are partly affirmative, partly negative.

6. In every real service it was required, that the two estates should be in distinct proprietors: whenever the owner of either became the owner of both, the service was extinct.

7. II. Personal services are rights, which are owing from an estate to a person. The principal of these are 1. Usufruct. 2. Use. 3. Habitation.

8. Usufruct is a right of using and enjoying the profits of a thing belonging to another, without impairing the substance.

9. An usufruct properly had place in such things only, as could be used without being consumed; but might be even in things which perished in the using, called RES FUNGIBILES.

10. If an usufructuary died ever so little before harvest, his estate, like that of an incumbent in England with regard to tithes, was immediately determined; and his heir had no right to the fruits: but if the usufructuary had sowed his land, the heir could deduct for seed and expence of tillage. A like indulgence is allowed to a tenant for life, by the laws of England.

11. Use is a right of using a thing belonging to another, for the purpose of supplying the daily wants and necessities of the user, without prejudice to the substance.

12. Habitation is a right to dwell in the house of another, without hurt to the building.

13. An use, in the law of England, is of as great extent as an usufruct in the Civil law; and he that hath the use of land hath the land itself: but our laws are silent concerning such uses and rights of habitation, as were among the Romans.

CHAPTER IV.

OF THE PERSONS, BY WHOM PROPERTY MIGHT BE ACQUIRED; AND OF THE PECULIUM OF A SON UNDER POWER.

Inst. Lib. II. Tit. 9.
Hoppii *Comm.* Lib. II. Tit. 9.
Heinecc. *A. R.* } Lib. II. Tit. 9.
——— *El. J. C.* }

Taylor's *El. of the Civ. Law.* art. *Power of the Father.* p. 395—397.

1. PROPERTY might be acquired not only immediately, by a man's self; but also mediately, by others whom he had under power; as a son and a slave.

2. Yet both a son and a slave were allowed to have some little property of their own, which was called peculium.

3. The peculium of a son was, 1. Military. 2. Pagan. The military peculium was, (1) *Castrense.* (2) *Quasi-Castrense.* The pagan peculium was, (1) *Profectitium.* (2) *Adventitium.*

4. Property might be acquired by means of a slave, in whom a man had only the usufruct.

CHAPTER V.

OF THE CIVIL MODES OF ACQUIRING PROPERTY; AND, FIRST, OF USUCAPION OR PRESCRIPTION; AND OF DONATION.

Inst. Lib. II. Tit. 6, 7.
Hoppii *Comm.* Lib. II. Tit. 6, 7.
Heinecc. *A. R.* } Lib. II. Tit. 6,
——— *El. J. C.* } 7.
Wood's *Inst. of the Civ. Law.* B. II. ch. 4.
Vinnii *Comm.* II. 6, 7.
Grotius *de J. B. et P.* Lib. II. ch. IV.
Wood's *Inst. of Laws of England.* B. II. ch. 3, 6.
Burn's *Ecc. Law.* Title, *Donatio mortis causa:* Title, *Wills.*
Blackstone's *Comm.* B. II. ch. 8. 17. 29. 30. B. III. ch. 20.

1. THE civil modes of acquiring a right to things, were, chiefly, three. I. Usucapion or Prescription. II. Donation. III. Succession[1].

[1] There is another distribution of the civil modes of acquiring a right to things, mentioned in the Institutions, into universal and singular. The universal modes are those, by which the whole rights of one man are transferred to another, in the gross, by one acquisition. These are six in number. 1. Hæreditas *tum ex testamento, tum ab intestato.* 2. Bonorum possessio. 3. *Acquisitio per* arrogationem. 4. Bonorum addictio libertatum servandarum causa. 5. *Acquisitio per* sectionem bonorum. 6. *Acquisitio ex* senatus-consulto Claudiano. The singular modes are those, by which the property of one single thing is transferred. These are four in number. 1. Usucapio. 2. Donatio. 3. Legatum. 4. Fidei-commissum singulare. This distribution is not without its use: but the division I have laid down is more commodious, and better adapted to the order, in which the several articles are treated of in the Institutions, than that of Justinian himself.

2. I. Usucapion was the acquisition of property, founded on continual possession, during a time expressed by law. Prescription was an *exception*, by which he, who had possessed a thing for a certain length of time, defended himself in the possession against the true owner.

3. Usucapion and prescription differed from each other, 1. In the things acquired. 2. In the time. 3. In the effect. These distinctions were abolished by Justinian; and prescription now comprehends the meaning of both terms.

4. In order to acquire a thing by prescription, the possession must be, 1. *Bona fide*. 2. Founded on a just cause or title. 3. Uninterrupted. 4. For a lawful time. 5. The thing itself must be capable of prescription.

5. The *Leges Atinia, Julia, Plotia;* and the alterations in the Decemviral law, made by Justinian; explained.

6. Services, and other incorporeal things, might be gained by prescription.

7. Prescriptions, in the law of England, are of two kinds. 1. Those which enable a man to acquire a property. 2. Those which secure him from loss and punishment.

8. By the common law of England the time of Prescription is that, of which there is no memory of man or record to the contrary: yet in many instances less time is sufficient, both by the common law, and by acts of parliament.

9. The maxim of the common law of England, with respect to the possessions of the Crown and

Church, expressed by the words, *Nullum tempus occurrit Regi vel Ecclesiæ;* and the statutes of limitation, (21 James I. c. 2. 9 Geo. III. c. 16. and 2 and 3 William IV. c. 100.) explained.

10. II. Donation is of two kinds. 1. Proper. 2. Improper.

11. A proper donation is, when one from mere liberality bestows any thing on another, not being compelled to it by law.

12. To the perfection of a gift were required, 1. The consent of the donor and donee. 2. Capacity in one to give, and the other to receive, 3. A capacity in the thing to be given. 4. Delivery. 5. Gifts, exceeding a certain sum, were to be publicly registered, at the time when made.

13. In the law of England, donation usually refers to real property, or to corporeal hereditaments; and signifies the conveyance of an estate-tail. The conveyance of an incorporeal hereditament is called a grant. In grants of personal property, an equivalent or consideration is always implied. Gifts are wholly gratuitous; and may be in word, in law, or by deed.

14. Gifts, perfectly made, might be recalled: 1. For ingratitude. 2. If inofficious. 3. In one case, if afterwards the giver had children. In England, gifts, made absolute, are irrecoverable.

15. Improper gifts are, 1. Those made *propter nuptias*. 2. *Mortis causa.*

16. A gift *propter nuptias* was a settlement, which the husband made on his wife, by way of security for her *dos*, or marriage portion. This *dos* was,

1. *Profectitia.* 2. *Adventitia.* The husband could not alienate his wife's *dos*, even with her consent.

17. In England, where a real estate is brought by the wife, the husband only gains a title to the rents and profits during coverture; unless, by the birth of a child, he become tenant for life *by the curtesy.* Chattels real are given to the husband conditionally, if he survives his wife; yet, while he lives, he can alienate them at pleasure. Chattels personal, if reduced *to possession*, are given to the husband absolutely, by the marriage; and the wife has property in nothing but her *paraphernalia*, or wearing apparel.

18. Dos, in the law of England, is not used to signify the money or land brought by the wife in marriage; but means that part of the husband's lands, (usually a third) which the wife has, by common law, after his decease.

19. Dower at common law may be barred. 1. By a settlement on the wife, previous to the marriage, which is called a jointure. 2. By the husband's disposition of the lands, by deed or by will. 3. By a declaration, either in the deed of conveyance of the lands, or in any other deed executed by the husband, that the wife shall not be entitled to dower out of such lands. 4. By a similar declaration in the husband's will, executed for the devise of freehold estates.

20. A gift *mortis causa* is one made in prospect or contemplation of death: in what respects this differs from a legacy. Donations of this kind are not unknown in England.

21. III. Succession is the right of coming into the estate, real or personal, which a deceased person had at the time of his death.

22. Such succession might take place three ways. I. By testament. II. By law. III. By the bonorum possessio granted by the prætor.

CHAPTER VI.

OF SUCCESSION BY TESTAMENT.

Inst. Lib. I. Tit. 10—19. Tit. 25.
Hoppii *Comm.* Lib. II. Tit. 10—19. Tit. 25.
Heinecc. *A. R.* Lib. II. Tit. 10—13. Tit. 14. Tit. 15, 16. Tit. 17—19. Tit. 23—25. §. 11—16.
——— *El. J. C.* Lib. II. Tit. 10—19. Tit. 25.
Wood's *Inst. of the Civ. Law.* Book II. ch. 4.
Taylor's *El. of the Civ. Law:* art. *Property.* p. 515—537.
Vinnii *Comm.* II. 10—19.
Wood's *Inst. of the Laws of England.* B. II. ch. 3, 6.
Burn's *Eccl. Law.* Title, *Wills.*
Blackstone's *Comm.* B. II. ch. 1, 23, 32.
Toller's *Law of Executors.*

1. PROPERTY naturally ceases at the death of the proprietor; but, by the law of many societies, may be continued by him, after his decease, in such persons as he shall expressly name.

2. A testament, in the Roman law, is the legal declaration of a man's intentions, which he wills to be performed upon the event of his death, with the direct appointment of an heir.

3. In England, the disposal of real property by a last will is called a devise; and the word testament, strictly speaking, is limited to the disposal of chattels or personal property, with the appointment of an executor.

4. In testaments are to be considered, I. Their original and antiquity. II. Their kinds. III. The persons capable of making a testament. IV. The things which a testament ought to contain, to make

it valid in law. V. The ways of avoiding a testament.

5. I. The power of making private testaments was not allowed among the Romans, till the laws of the Twelve Tables.

6. The power of devising lands subsisted in England before the conquest, and till about the reign of Henry II. when it, generally, ceased, in consequence of the feudal tenures: the Doctrine of Uses revived this power; and the Statute of Uses (27 Hen. VIII. c. 10.) again, accidentally, checked it: this occasioned the Statute of Wills, (32 Hen. VIII. c. 1, and 34. c. 5.) which expressly conferred the right of devising, but with some restrictions with regard to lands held by knight's service: the alterations of tenures in the reign of Charles II. abolished these restrictions; and the power of devising was then made to extend to the whole of a man's landed property. The disposition of copyhold estates is regulated by 55 Geo. III. c. 192.

7. By the Common Law of England, a man could only bequeath one third of his personal estate by testament; the other two thirds being reserved for his wife and children; whose shares were called their *reasonable part:* but by modern statutes, a man may now bequeath the whole of his chattels, as freely as he can devise the whole of his landed property.

8. II. Before the laws of the Twelve Tables, a testamentary heir might be made two ways. 1. In the form of a legislative act, Comitiis Calatis. 2. In procinctu, by such persons as belonged to the army.

9. The Twelve Tables gave an absolute power to every man, to make the law of his own succession; but prescribed no *form*.

10. As a testament was an alienation of the testator's property and family after his death, the form of mancipation, used in other transfers of property or family, was followed in this; which occasioned a third kind of testament, *per æs et libram*.

11. Afterwards, when testaments came to be in writing, the prætor took away the ceremony of the symbolical sale; requiring no more to the validity of a Will than seven witnesses, (instead of five required before) and their seals: this was called *testamentum prætorium*.

12. This regulation was followed by another and the last, from which was formed the *Testamentum* Mixtum; so called, because made up of three sorts of law, the Civil and the Prætorian Law, and the Constitutions of the Emperors.

13. A Roman testament was, 1. Solemn. 2. Privileged: and both were either written, or nuncupative. The solemnities were, 1. External. 2. Internal.

14. In a solemn written testament it was required, that it should be, 1. written, or subscribed, by the testator. 2. Subscribed, and sealed, by seven persons, all freemen, citizens of Rome, fourteen years of age at least, in the sight and hearing of the testator, and solemnly required to bear witness. 3. That the whole should be done *uno contextu*.

15. The *condition*, or positive capacity, of the witnesses was to be judged of, at the time of their attestation; yet, by an equitable construction, general reputation was sufficient.

16. Neither the heir, nor any of his family, could be witnesses; but legatees, and *fide-committees*, might.

17. The omission of any solemnity in a written unprivileged will made the whole invalid. Whether, in case of a will defective in form, the heir at law be bound in conscience to restore the inheritance to the testamentary heir; examined.

18. In devises of real estates in England, it is required that they be, 1. In writing, signed by the devisor himself, or some other in his presence, and by his direction. 2. Subscribed by three credible witnesses at least, in presence of the devisor. A legacy given in such a will to any of the witnesses, is void; and the will itself, in other respects, is good: but creditors are held to be credible witnesses, though the real estate be charged with payment of debts[1]*.

19. Testaments of chattels in England, if written in the testators own hand, without his name, or seal, or witnesses present; and even if written in another hand, and never signed by the testator, if proved to have been agreeable to his instructions; are good.

[1] See the Act of 25 Geo. II. c. 6. and the case of Windham *versus* Chetwynd, 31 Geo. II. 1757, in Burrow's Reports, Vol. I. p. 414. with the opinion of the Court of King's Bench, delivered by Lord Mansfield; where the regulation of the English and Roman Laws, concerning testaments in general, and the credibility of witnesses to testaments in particular, are explained at large, with an erudition and accuracy, peculiar to that great lawyer.

* Freehold and copyhold estates of deceased persons are made liable to the payment of debts due on simple contract and on specialty by 3 and 4 Will. IV. c. 104.

20. A distinction is made between devises and testaments with regard to after acquired property; a testament will operate upon all such personal estates as a testator dies possessed of, at whatever distance of time he may die after making the testament; but a devise of real estate will operate on such estates only as were his at the time of executing and publishing his will.

21. In a solemn nuncupative testament it was required, that the testator should declare his will, by word of mouth, before seven witnesses, specially asked to attest it.

22. In England, no nuncupative will is good, where the estate bequeathed exceeds thirty pounds, unless, 1. Made in the last sickness of the testator. 2. At his own house; except surprised by illness, when abroad. 3. Proved by three persons present, specially required to bear witness. 4. Put into writing, within six days from the making, if proved by the witnesses after six months. Nor will a nuncupative will revoke a precedent written one, unless reduced to writing in the life time of the testator, and read over to him, and approved.

23. Privileged testaments were those, which were valid without the formalities required in such as were solemn. Among these, the military testament was the chief.

24. The privilege of unsolemn testaments granted to soldiers extended only to such as were in actual service: and a will so made continued in force a whole year after their dismission from the army.

25. Soldiers and sailors, in England, have the privilege of making informal testaments.

26. Other instances of privileged testaments were, 1. Those that were publicly registered. 2. Those made by parents for the benefit of their children. 3. By rustics. 4. In time of a plague. 5. For pious causes. In England, several charitable devises have been adjudged good as *appointments*, which were not valid as testamentary dispositions.

27. Codicils were unsolemn wills, which contained no appointment of an heir; and might be made by one that died testate or intestate.

28. Codicils differed from testaments, 1. In their formalities. 2. In their use. In England, the distinction between them is little more than nominal.

29. A will defective in form might often be supported by the force of a codicillary clause: in England, such a clause is of no use.

30. Codicils in England are either written or nuncupative; and, when regularly attested and executed, may be proved as wills are.

31. III. All persons are capable of making a testament, unless disabled, 1. By their state and condition. 2. Want of discretion. 3. Criminal conduct.

32. Persons disabled by their state and condition were, 1. A son under power. 2. Slaves. 3. Strangers. 4. Deaf and dumb persons. 5. Prisoners of war, during their captivity: but a will made before captivity was good, whether the captive returned, or died with the enemy.

33. In England, the power of a father is no impediment to a child's testament: but the power of a husband will vitiate a wife's testament of chat-

tels, unless made by his consent; she may, with her husband's concurrence, dispose of lands, and money subject to be invested in the purchase of lands, according to the directions of 3 and 4 William IV. c. 74, § 77—80.

34. Persons disabled by want of discretion were, 1. Those under the age of puberty. 2. Madmen. 3. Prodigals.

35. In England, a male of fourteen years of age, and a female of twelve, may make a will of a personal estate; but neither of them can devise lands till the age of twenty-one.

36. Persons disabled by criminal conduct were, 1. Traitors. 2. Hereticks. 3. Incestuous. 4. Libellers, &c. Certain criminous persons are incapable of making a testament, in England.

37. IV. The appointment of an heir to represent the testator was an *internal* solemnity, which made the essence of a Roman testament.

38. He is called heir, in the Civil Law, who succeeds to the *whole* estate of the deceased, real or personal, without distinction. By the law of England, he is properly heir, who succeeds to the *real* estate, by right of *blood;* and he that succeeds to the *personal* estate, by *will,* is called executor.

39. There were three kinds of heirs, in the Roman law. 1. Necessarii. 2. Sui et necessarii. 3. Extranei. In England, all persons are capable of being executors, who are capable of making wills, and many others besides.

40. Necessary heirs were the testator's slaves. Effects of the appointment of a slave for heir, in

the cases of *Servus proprius*, *alienus*, *communis*, *hæreditarius*.

41. *Hæredes* SUI ET NECESSARII were all the children of the testator, of whatever sex or degree, born or posthumous.

42. By the old Civil Law, if a father neither instituted his son heir, nor disinherited him *by name*, the will was void: but the same omission, in the case of a daughter, or of a grandson by a son or by a daughter, did not hurt the will.

43. Posthumous children were of three sorts. 1. *Sui*. 2. *Alieni*. 3. *Quasi posthumi*.

44. The birth of a posthumous son or daughter; (which was called *Agnatio sui hæredis*) or of a grandson born after the death of the grandfather, and succeeding into the place of his father; (which was called *Quasi-Agnatio sui hæredis*) would regularly have voided the will of a parent, which was good at the time when made. The form, contrived by *Gallus Aquilius*, by which such a grandson might be instituted *conditionally*[1]; and the *Lex Julia Vellæa*, with regard to the institution of the *Quasi-posthumi*; explained.

45. In the disinherison of posthumous children, the males were to be disinherited *by name*; and females *inter cæteros*, with a legacy.

46. By the new law, as reformed by Justinian, all children, of whatever sex or degree, born or posthumous, were to be instituted or disinherited *by name*.

[1] The form was this: *Filius meus hæres esto. Si filius meus vivo me morietur, tunc, si quis mihi ex eo nepos, post mortem meam, in decem mensibus proximis quibus filius meus moreretur, natus erit, hæres esto.* See D. 28. 2. 29.

47. In England, a testator may omit or exclude his own children by his will, and appoint others to be his heirs or executors, as he pleases: nor does the birth of a posthumous child at all affect the will of a father. But marriage and the birth of a child amount to a revocation.

48. Extraneous heirs were all those, who were neither the slaves, nor the children of the testator: these were sometimes called *voluntary* heirs.

49. Those only could be extraneous heirs, who had a capacity to accept the inheritance, both at the time of making the will, and at the time of the testator's death.

50. A testator might institute one heir, or more heirs than one: but no person, except a soldier, by the Roman law, could die partly testate, and partly intestate.

51. Where one heir only was instituted, he succeeded to the whole inheritance, whether he were instituted simply, or to a part. The whole inheritance was called A S; its divisions and subdivisions explained.

52. When a testator instituted more heirs than one, he might, 1. Institute them all simply. 2. Institute some with parts, some without. 3. Allot to each his respective part.

53. The institution of heirs might be absolute, or conditional. Conditions were, 1. Casual. 2. Potestative. 3. Mixt: and were further divided into possible and impossible.

54. An heir could not be instituted *from* a certain time, or *till* a certain time: but this law does not obtain in England, with regard to an Executor.

55. An heir was obliged to make some *declaration* of his accepting of the inheritance.

56. By the old law, the heir was bound to acquit all the burthens of the inheritance, if he once accepted; and therefore had a certain time allowed to *deliberate*, whether he would take on him the office or not: and this indulgence, by favour of the prætor, was extended even to the *sui hæredes* of the testator.

57. The time of deliberating was afterwards superseded by the method of making an *inventory*, introduced by Justinian; by which the heir was not bound to creditors *ultra vires hæreditarias*. This method is followed in England with regard to executors: and until an inventory be made, it will be presumed, the testator hath left *assets* sufficient to pay every debt.

58. An executor in England, after making an inventory, is obliged to prove the will, either in *common form*, or *per testes*. The manner of proving it, and the persons impowered to grant the *probate;* explained.

59. An executor, after once intermeddling with the estate of the testator, cannot renounce his executorship; but is not liable *de bonis propriis* to pay more than he has received.

60. Before inventories were introduced, the office of an heir was sometimes refused as dangerous: and upon this foresight substitutions, or conditional institutions, were created. These were, 1. Vulgar. 2. Pupillar. 3. Quasi-pupillar.

61. The vulgar substitution was the appointment of a second or third heir, in failure of the

first[1]. If the first accepted, none of the substitutes could succeed.

62. There might be several substitutes in the place of one instituted; or one substitute in the place of several instituted; or the persons substituted might be the same with those who were instituted.

63. In a reciprocal substitution, if the testator had omitted to express the parts, into which he divided the inheritance, they were understood to be the same he had expressed in the institution.

64. The pupillar substitution was, when a father substituted an heir to his children under power, disposing of his own estate and theirs, in case the child refused to accept the inheritance, or died before the age of puberty[2]. The father and child under puberty were esteemed but one person; and therefore one will, or testament, served for both.

65. The vulgar substitution expressed contained the pupillar; and the pupillar substitution expressed contained the vulgar[3].

[1] The condition of the vulgar substitution was, *Si institutus hæres non erit:* and it was expressed in this form, *Titius hæres esto: si titius hæres non erit, tunc seius esto.*

[2] The condition of the pupillar substitution was, *Si filius hæres erit et intra pubertatem decesserit:* and the form of expressing that condition was, *Filius meus hæres esto: si filius meus hæres non erit; sive hæres erit, et prius moriatur quam in suam tutelam venerit; tunc seius hæres esto.*

[3] In other words, the vulgar form, *Si filius hæres non erit,* comprehended the pupillar, *Si filius hæres erit et intra pubertatem decesserit:* and the pupillar form, *Si filius hæres erit et intra pubertatem decesserit,* comprehended the vulgar, *Si filius hæres non erit.* The latter part of the proposition, before it became an established maxim of the Civil Law, was the subject of a memorable dispute, in the cause of Curius and Coponius,

66. No one by substitution could make a testament for his child, unless he first made a testament for himself; and if the father's testament became void, that for his son was void also.

67. The quasi-pupillar substitution related to those children, who were past puberty, but unable, on account of some infirmity of mind or body, to make a testament for themselves; for whom therefore the parent was impowered to make a testament, after the *example* of the pupillar substitution.

68. Entailed estates in England resemble, in some respects, the substitutions of the Roman law.

69. V. Testaments might be avoided, 1. By law. 2. By the office of the judge. The difference between *testamentum nullum, destitutum, ruptum, irritum;* explained. A testament became void by law, when it was either *ruptum* or *irritum.*

70. A testament was *broken,* 1. By the agnation, or *quasi*-agnation[4] of a *Suus Hæres.* 2. By a change of will in the testator.

between two of the greatest lawyers of their time, Q. Scævola and L. Licinius Crassus. It may not be without its use to subjoin the case itself; as it is related by Cicero, in his Treatise De Oratore, I. 39. *Clarissima M. Curii causa M. que Coponii, nuper apud Centumviros, quo concursu hominum, qua expectatione defensa est? cum Q. Scævola*—ex scripto *testamentorum jura defenderet, negaretque, nisi posthumus* et natus, et ante, quam in suam tutelam venisset, mortuus esset, *Hæredem* eum *esse posse, qui esset secundum posthumum* et *natum* et *mortuum hæres institutus: Ego* voluntatem *defenderem, hac eum tum mente fuisse qui testamentum fecisset, ut si filius* non *esset qui in tutelam veniret, M. Curius esset Hæres. Num destitit uterque nostrum in ea causa, in auctoritatibus, in exemplis, in testamentorum formulis, hoc est, in medio Jure Civili, versari?*

[4] See Prop. 44.

71. A change of will in the testator might be declared two ways. 1. By cancelling or destroying a former testament. 2. By making a new one of later date.

72. If the latter testament, revoking the former, was not *perfect* in its kind, the former still continued good. In England, wills, which concern a personal estate, though not finished, *may* be good as to the things already bequeathed: but a devise in writing cannot be revoked, otherwise than by some other will or writing, signed by three witnesses. Marriage and the birth of a child are an implied revocation.

73. A testament became *ineffectual*, on account of some change of state in the testator.

74. A testament, good at the time of making, may become void by a change of state, or alteration of circumstances in the testator, by the English laws.

75. A testament, *broken* or *ineffectual* by *the* CIVIL LAW, was often supported by the Law of the Prætor.

76. A testament became void by the office of the judge, by the action called *Querela inofficiosi Testamenti*. The cases, in which this action had place, and the regulations concerning it, made by Justinian; explained.

77. If a child could come at his father's inheritance any other way, this was a bar to the *querela*.

78. No such action as the *querela* subsists in England: what most resembled it, was the writ called *Breve de rationabili parte bonorum*, which

the wife or children of a deceased testator had against executors, for recovery of part of the goods. A man may now bequeath his personal property as he pleases[1]. But the custom of reserving a reasonable part for widows and children is still in force in the city of London, and in the province of York, when a man dies intestate.

[1] See Prop. 7.

CHAPTER VII.

OF LEGACIES.

Inst. Lib. II. Tit. 20—22.
Hoppii *Comm.* Lib. II. Tit. 20—22.
Heinecc. *A. R.* / ——— *El. J. C.* } Lib. II. Tit. 20—22.
Wood's *Inst. of the Civ. Law.* B. II. ch. 4.
Vinnii *Comm.* II. 20.

Wood's *Inst. of Laws of England.* B. II. ch. 6.
Burn's *Eccl. Law.* Title, *Wills.* art. *Payment of Legacies.*
Blackstone's *Comm.* B. II. ch. 18. 32.
Toller's *Law of Executors.*

1. A LEGACY is a bequest or gift of goods, left by the testator, to be delivered by the heir.

2. By the old Civil Law there were four kinds of legacies; *per Vindicationem, Damnationem, Præceptionem, Sinendi modo;* to each of which was assigned a certain form of words: but these distinctions were taken away by Justinian, and legacies were all reduced to one kind.

3. In legacies are to be considered, I. The things capable of being left as legacies. II. The persons capable of receiving them. III. The effects and incidents of legacies. IV. The ways by which they might be extinguished.

4. I. Things corporeal, or incorporeal, existing at present, or in futurity, belonging to the testator, or to any other person, might be left as legacies.

5. *Legatum liberationis, nominis, generis, optionis, Pœnæ nomine;* explained.

6. If a legacy was lost or perished before delivery, without the fault of the heir, the loss was to

the legatee; if by the fault of the heir, he was bound to make it good.

7. II. All persons were capable of receiving legacies, who could either make a testament, or receive from the testament of another.

8. A legacy to a posthumous child was good; as also to an uncertain person, provided the person designed by the testator could be discovered.

9. An error in the proper name or sirname of the legatee, or a false description or cause added to a legacy, did not make it void.

10. A legacy to a company or corporation was good. How far such legacies are restrained by the Statutes of *Mortmain*, in England, explained.

11. Certain persons are incapable of legacies, by the laws of England.

12. III. By the old law, no legacies left in a testament were effectual, unless the testator had first appointed an heir; but this order was no longer necessary, after the times of Justinian.

13. In what cases the *Jus Accrescendi* (called, in England, the right of Survivorship) had place among co-legatees; explained.

14. A legacy might be left purely, or conditionally; to a certain day, or from a certain day.

15. In England, if a legatee die before the testator, the legacy is *lapsed*. In *contingent* legacies, when the time is joined to the *substance* of the legacy, and the legatee dies before the day; it is a lapsed legacy: when the time is joined to the *payment*, it is a *vested* legacy; and if the legatee die before the day, his right is transmitted to his representatives.

16. In what cases, and from what time, a legacy shall bear interest, by the English laws.

17. A testator was not permitted to exhaust his whole patrimony in legacies, and leave nothing for his testamentary heir. The *leges furia, voconia, falcidia,* explained.

18. By this last law, a testator could not give away in legacies more than three parts in four of his estate: the fourth part, thus secured to the heir, was called the *falcidian* portion.

19. The *falcidian* portion was estimated, according to the value of the inheritance at the time of the testator's death, after the funeral expences and debts were paid.

20. In England, when there is a deficiency of *assets,* all general legacies must abate proportionably, in order to pay the debts of the testator; and the legatees, if paid their legacies, are obliged to refund.

21. IV. Legacies were extinguished, 1. By ademption. 2. By translation.

CHAPTER VIII.

OF FIDEI-COMMISSA, OR BEQUESTS IN TRUST.

Inst. Lib. II. Tit. 23, 24.
Hoppii *Comm.* Lib. II. Tit. 23, 24.
Heinecc. *A. R.* Lib. II. Tit. 23—25. pr. § 1—10.
——— *El. J. C.* Lib. II. Tit. 23—24.
Wood's *Inst. of the Civ. Law.* B. II. ch. 4.
Blackstone's *Comm.* B. II. ch. 20.

1. FIDEI-COMMISSA, or bequests in trust, were, I. Universal. II. Particular.

2. I. An universal *fidei-commissum* was the disposal of an inheritance, in whole or in part, to an heir, *in trust* that he should convey it, or dispose of the profits of it, to another. He, to whom the inheritance was given in trust, was called *hæres fiduciarius;* he, who had a beneficial interest in the inheritance, was called *hæres fidei-commissarius.*

3. To prevent the fiduciary heir from being bound to the creditors of the deceased testator, it was provided by the *sctum trebellianum*, that all the actions, which by the Civil Law might be brought by or against the fiduciary heir, should be transferred to the *fide-committee.*

4. But as bequests in trust were still liable to be defeated, by the fiduciary heir refusing to accept, the *sctum pegasianum* was made; by which, after the example of the *falcidian* law with regard to

legacies, the fiduciary heir was permitted to retain a fourth part of the inheritance, if instituted universal heir; or a fourth of his portion, if instituted heir for a part.

5. These two *scta* were afterwards reduced into one, by Justinian.

6. A bequest *in trust* might be left by codicil or by testament.

7. II. A particular *fidei-commissum* was the disposal of one particular thing to an heir, *in trust* that he should deliver it to another.

8. Such a particular *fidei-commissum* differed little from a legacy.

9. Estates vested in trustees for the benefit of a third party; and what are called uses and trusts in the laws of England; are, in many respects, similar to the fiduciary settlements of the Roman Law.

CHAPTER IX.

OF SUCCESSION BY LAW.

Wood's *Inst. of the Civ. Law*. B. II. ch. 4.
Burn's *Eccl. Law*. Title, *Wills*. art. *Administration*.
Blackstone's *Comm*. B. II. ch. 1. 14. 32.

1. IN cases, where a person hath neglected, or was not permitted to dispose of his property, after his decease, by testament; the law of each particular society appoints a successor, whom it judges to have the best right to enter on the vacant possession.

2. Succession by law is the title, by which a man, on the death of his ancestor, dying intestate, acquires his estate, whether real or personal, by the right of representation, as his next heir.

3. An intestate is one, who dies without a will; or who leaves a will, which is not valid.

4. In England, succession by law to an estate in lands is called descent; the person succeeding is called the heir; and the estate itself is called the inheritance. In succession by law to an estate in goods, the persons, in whom they were formerly vested, were the Bishops, by indulgence of the King: but Bishops are now compelled to commit

their power to certain persons called administrators, expressly provided by law.

5. Succession by law is of two sorts. 1. *In capita*, when the inheritance is divided *viritim*, according to the number of persons; all claiming in *their own* right, as being in equal degree of kindred. 2. *In stirpes*, when the inheritance is divided *gregatim;* the claimants being supposed to come, by right of *representation*, into the place of the person deceased, and dividing that share in common, which he, whom they represent, would have had, had he been living.

6. The Roman law, concerning intestate succession, which is contained in the Institutions, was entirely defeated by the Novels.

I.

OF SUCCESSION BY LAW, ACCORDING TO THE INSTITUTIONS.

Inst. Lib. III. Tit. 1—6.
Heinecc. *A. R.* } Lib. III. Tit.
——— *El. J. C.* } 1—6.

Esprit des Loix. Liv. XXVII.
Blackstone's *Comm.* B. II. ch. 14. 15.

7. THE old Roman law concerning successions is to be explained from the law concerning the division of lands; which required that the property of one family should not pass into another.

8. The old Roman law acknowledged only two orders in the succession to an intestate estate. I. The *sui.* II. The *agnati.* To these was added, by the prætor, a third. III. The order of *cognati.*

9. I. The *sui* were such children as were, 1. In the family, and under the power, of their father. 2. In the first degree.

10. Children born in concubinage, when legitimated, were reckoned *sui hæredes.*

11. Emancipated children, though excluded from the *suitas* by the Civil Law, were restored to it by the law of the prætor.

12. Adopted children, by a constitution of Justinian, belonged to the family, and were under the power, of their natural father; and were only so far of the family of their adoptive father, as to succeed to his goods with his other children, if he died intestate.

13. It was indifferent, whether the *suus hæres* were male or female: sons and daughters succeeded in their own right, *in capita;* grandchildren from a *son,* though in ever so remote a degree, succeeded, by right of representation, *in stirpes.*

14. Grandchildren from a *daughter* were not *sui hæredes:* but the constitutions of the emperors gave them the rights of the *suitas,* and put them, nearly, on the same foot with grandchildren from a son.

15. II. In default of a *suus hæres,* the law of the Twelve Tables passed to the collateral line, and called in the *agnati.*

16. *Agnati* were those relations, male and female, which came from the same father, though from different mothers.

17. The Decemviral Law, in calling the *agnati* to an intestate inheritance, made no distinction of sex: the *Media Jurisprudentia* excluded women,

beyond such sisters as were *consanguineæ:* Justinian permitted all the *agnati*, whether male or female, to inherit, according to the prerogative of degree; and made the *soror uterina* equal to the *soror germana*.

18. The rights of agnation were given by Justinian to sisters' children, if the intestate left no brother or sister living; but did not extend to sisters' grandchildren.

19. If the first degree failed, by death or renunciation, the inheritance was not transmissible to the next, till the times of Justinian.

20. In the collateral line, the right of *representation* did not take place; but the nearest degree, whether one or more, excluded all the remoter; and the succession was always *in capita*.

21. Agnatic succession has place in *descents*, by the laws of England; which, in collateral inheritances, always prefer the male stocks before the female, unless where lands have actually descended from a female.

22. The law of the Twelve Tables did not allow inheritances to *ascend*. A father could succeed to his son, whom he had emancipated: but this succession was founded on the ancient ceremony of emancipation; by which the parent was considered as a *quasi-patronus*, and the child as his *quasi-libertus*[1].

23. A mother and her child could not succeed each other by the Decemviral Law. The *sctum Tertullianum* permitted a mother, that had a certain

[1] See Book I. Ch. 9. pr. 13.

number of children, to succeed to a son or a daughter, who had left no children of their own; but did not allow her to succeed to a grandson or a granddaughter.

24. If the intestate child left a father *and* a mother, the father was preferred: if a father and mother, together with a grandfather, the grandfather was preferred to the other two: if a mother and grandfather only, the grandfather was excluded.

25. Brothers and sisters by the whole blood, and brothers by the same father, excluded the mother; sisters by the same father were admitted with the mother: if there were both brothers and sisters, the inheritance was equally divided between them, and the mother was excluded.

26. The regulations in the *sctum Tertullianum,* made by Justinian, explained.

27. The *sctum orficianum* called a child, whether son or daughter, to the inheritance of the mother; as the *sctum Tertullianum* had called the mother to the inheritance of her child: and this privilege was extended, by the Constitutions, to grandchildren, with regard to their grandmother.

28. Natural children, and spurious, were equally favoured by the *sctum orficianum,* with those that were legitimate.

29. The issue of bastards is sometimes favoured, as to real estates, by the laws of England.

30. III. When both the orders of *sui* and *agnati* failed, whether reckoned by the laws of the Twelve Tables, or of the Senate, or by the Constitutions; the prætor introduced his third order of *cognati.*

31. *Cognati* were those relations, male and female, which came by the mother.

32. The rights of cognation were given, by the Prætorian Law, 1. To such as had once the right of agnation, but lost it by a change of family. 2. To such as never had that right, being descended from the mother. 3. To spurious children.

II.

OF SUCCESSION BY LAW, ACCORDING TO THE NOVELS.

Novell. CXVIII. Cap. 1. 2. 3.
——— CXXVII. Cap. 1.
Institutions of Justinian by Dr. Harris: with Nov. CXVIII. Cap. 1. 2. 3. at the end.
Hoppii *Comm.* Lib. III. *Tabulæ de Successione ab Intestato.*
Heinecc. *El. J. C.* Lib. III. *De Successione ab Intestato, secundum Nov.* CXVIII.
Wood's *Inst. of the Civ. Law.* B. II. ch. 4.
Taylor's *El. of the Civ. Law.* art. *Property,* p. 537—544.
Wood's *Inst. of the Laws of England.* B. II. ch. 3. 6.
Burn's *Eccl. Law.* Title, *Wills,* art. *Distribution.*
Blackstone's *Comm.* B. II. ch. 8. 14. 15. 52.
Irving's *Observations on the Civil Law.*

33. In succession by law, as settled by Justinian in the Novels, the distinctions between the *sui* and *emancipati,* and between the *agnati* and *cognati,* were abolished.

34. The orders of succession, according to the Novels, were three. I. Descendants. II. Ascendants. III. Collaterals.

35. The courts in England, which have cognizance of the distribution of intestates effects, in cases where our laws are silent, or not sufficiently express, are chiefly guided by the doctrine of the Novels.

36. I. Descendants, of whatever degree, male or female, excluded all other relations, whether ascendants or collaterals.

37. By the law of England, inheritances lineally descend, to the issue of the person last seized, *in infinitum*. In the distribution of goods, the Statute Law gives the same preference with the Civil Law to descendants, exclusive of ascendants and collaterals; only taking in the wife of the deceased, where there is one surviving.

38. Sons and daughters, that is, the immediate descendants of the deceased, succeeded *in capita:* in failure of them, descendants of a more remote degree succeeded, by representation, *in stirpes;* whether they were alone, or had uncles to concur with them.

39. In succession to lands, in England, the lineal descendants, *in infinitum*, of a person deceased, represent their ancestor. In succession to goods, where all the claimants in the right line are in *equal* degree, the division of the estate is *in capita;* and *representation* is only then introduced, when necessary to prevent exclusion.

40. A child in the mother's womb was reckoned among the descendants of the deceased, by the Civil Law. In England, distribution is not made till within one year from the death of the intestate; within which time, all posthumous children will be born.

41. In the order of descendants, no regard was had to primogeniture; and no preference in respect to sex.

42. In England, with regard to lands, the male issue is admitted before the female: where there are two or more males in equal degree, the eldest only inherits; but the females all together.

43. In the distribution of goods of an intestate in England, one third goes to the widow, and the remainder, in equal portions, to his children, or to their representatives: if no widow, all is distributed among the children: if no children or representatives, a moiety goes to the widow, and the other moiety to the *next of kin*, in equal degree, and their representatives.

44. The degrees of consanguinity, by which the next of kin are investigated, are reckoned, in the distribution of goods in England, according to the computation of the Civil Law.

45. II. When an intestate left no descendants, and no collaterals; such ascendants as were nearest in degree, male or female, paternal or maternal, succeeded to his estate, to the exclusion of all the remoter; for, among ascendants, representation was not admitted.

46. When several ascendants concurred in the same degree, those on the part of the father received a moiety, and those on the part of the mother had the other moiety; without regard to the number of persons on either side.

47. If besides a father or mother, who are ascendants nearest in degree, there were also collaterals, as brothers and sisters of the whole blood, all succeeded in equal portions, *in capita:* but brothers'

and sisters' children, if of the whole blood succeeded, by representation only, *in stirpes*[1]. Brothers or sisters of the half blood, and brothers' or sisters' grandchildren, were totally excluded.

48. If there was no father or mother, but a grandfather and a brother or sister of the whole blood, *whether* such brother or sister excluded the grandfather; examined[2].

49. In succession to lands in England, inheritances never could ascend: but lands, which came by the father, *descended* to the heirs on the part of the father; and lands, which came by the mother, to the heirs on the part of the mother. It is enacted by 3 and 4 William IV. c. 106. § 6. that every lineal ancestor shall be *capable* of being heir to any of his issue.

50. In the distribution of goods in England, when a child dies intestate, leaving a father, but no children of his own; the father is entitled to the whole: if he leaves no father, but a mother, toge-

[1] It may be proper here to remark, that this attention to brothers' and sisters' children was not in consequence of Nov. 118. cap. 2. but of one yet later, *viz.* Nov. 127. cap. 1.

[2] The words of Nov. 118. c. 2. are, *Si verò cum ascendentibus inveniantur fratres aut sorores ex utrisque parentibus conjuncti defuncto, cum proximis gradu ascendentibus vocabuntur, si et pater aut mater fuerint.* And the generality of commentators have understood this passage as admitting ascendants, whether the *next in degree* or not, and brothers, to take *jointly*. *Voet* supports the contrary opinion; and the Lord Chancellor Hardwicke, in a learned argument, as his manner was, on the case of *Evelyn* and *Evelyn*, adopted *Voet's* interpretation, and declared in favour of the brother, to the *exclusion* of the grandfather. See *Voet* comment. ad Pandectas, Vol. II. Lib. 38. Tit. 17. § 13. and Burn's Ecclesiastical Law. Title, *Wills: Distribution.*

ther with brothers or sisters, or their representatives, every brother and sister, and their representatives, have an equal share with her: grandfathers and grandmothers are admitted, in exclusion of uncles and aunts: ascendants, equal in degree, succeed to equal shares.

51. III. In the order of collaterals, when no one was left in the descending or ascending lines, there might be, 1. Brothers and sisters alone. 2. Brothers and sisters, together with brothers' and sisters' children. 3. Brothers' and sisters' children alone.

52. Brothers and sisters alone, of the whole blood, succeeded *in capita,* to the exclusion of the half blood: brothers' and sisters' children, concurring with brothers and sisters, succeeded, by representation, *in stirpes:* brothers' and sisters' children, alone, succeeded *in capita.*

53. No representatives were admitted among collaterals, after brothers' and sisters' children.

54. In default of the whole blood, the half succeeded.

55. If there were neither brothers nor sisters, nor their children; other collaterals were called in, according to the prerogative of degree: and if several were found in the same degree: all succeeded *in capita.*

56. In descents in England, the whole blood *was* preferred, and the half blood *was* entirely excluded: which might sometimes have debarred a son from an inheritance, descended from his own father.

57. It is enacted by 3 and 4 William IV. c. 106. § 9. that any person related to the person

from whom the descent is to be traced by the half blood shall be *capable* of being his heir.

58. In the distribution of goods in England, brothers and sisters, whether of the whole or half blood, being in *equal* degree to the intestate, are entitled to equal shares of his estate: brothers' and sisters' children, concurring with brothers and sisters, succeeded *in stirpes:* brothers' and sisters' children, alone, succeed *in capita:* and no representation is admitted, beyond brothers' and sisters' children.

59. By the law of the code[1], if no one was left in the descending, ascending, or collateral lines, the husband succeeded to the estate of the wife, and the wife to the estate of the husband. The law of the Novels[2] directs that the survivor shall have a portion, in certain cases where the deceased has left relatives.

60. In England, provision is made for widows, by *dower* or *jointure;* and a husband, who has married a woman seized of an estate of inheritance, and has issue by her, born alive, is, on the death of his wife, tenant for life *by the curtesy.*

61. Lastly, in default of a legal heir, the estate became a *res caduca*, and the *fiscus*, or exchequer, succeeded. In England also, upon deficiency of inheritable blood, lands *escheat* to the King, or to the Lord of whom they are holden.

[1] C. 6. 18. 1. [2] Nov. 53. c. 6. Nov. 74. c. 5. Nov. 117. c. 5.

CHAPTER X.

OF THE SUCCESSION OF THE LIBERTI.

Inst. Lib. III. Tit. 7, 8, 9.	Heinecc. *A. R.* / ——— *El. J. C.*	Lib. III. Tit. 7, 8, 9.

1. BY the old law, slaves, even after manumission, had no right to inherit from each other. The Emperor Valentinian permitted the children and grandchildren of a *libertus* to succeed to him, dying intestate; and this privilege was extended by Justinian to all his descendants, in exclusion of the right of the patron.

2. By the Decemviral Law, a libertus might securely pass his patron by, in his last will; and, in case of intestacy, the patron then only succeeded, if the libertus left no such children as had the *jus suitatis*.

3. The law of the prætor restrained the libertus from passing his patron by, in his last will; and gave the patron *possession of the goods*, as far as a moiety, if the libertus, having no *suus hæres* of his own, had left him less than that sum.

4. The *Lex Papia Poppæa* afterwards enacted, that, whether the libertus died testate or intestate, provided he were of the richer sort, and left less than three children, the patron should be admitted to a *pars virilis*.

5. The regulations in the Prætorian Law, and in the *Lex Papia Poppæa*, made by Justinian; explained.

6. The patron being dead, his children, in the nearest degree, succeeded to the goods of the libertus: unless the patron, by his last will, or otherwise, had *assigned* the libertus to any one child, in preference to the rest; in which case such child alone had the *jus patronatus*, and the other children were excluded.

CHAPTER XI.

OF SUCCESSION BY THE BONORUM POSSESSIO GRANTED BY THE PRÆTOR.

Inst. Lib. III. Tit. 10.	Heinecc. *A. R.* } Lib. III. Tit. 10.
Hoppii *Comm.* Lib. III. Tit. 10.	——— *El. J. C.* } Lib. III. Tit. 10.
	Vinnii *Comm.* III. 10.

1. Bonorum *possessio* is the right of pursuing and retaining the inheritance of a person deceased, not strictly due by the Civil Law, but granted by the prætor, from a principle of equity.

2. The *bonorum possessio,* granted by the prætor, was, 1. Edictal, or ordinary; when the cause was not heard judicially. 2. Decretal, or extraordinary; when the cause was heard judicially.

3. The edictal or ordinary grant took place, 1. When there was a testament. 2. When there was not a testament.

4. The ordinary grant, when there *was* a testament, was, 1. *Contra tabulas,* in favour of children passed by in the testament, without just cause. 2. *Secundum tabulas,* to support a testament defective in form.

5. The ordinary grant, when there was *not* a testament, was reduced by Justinian to four kinds. 1. *Unde liberi,* in favour of emancipated children. 2. *Unde legitimi,* in favour of the *agnati.* 3. *Unde*

cognati, given to relations on the part of the mother. 4. *Unde vir et uxor*, by which the husband and wife succeeded each other, when the *cognati* failed.

6. The decretal or extraordinary grant was given to particular persons, by a special law or constitution.

7. The *bonorum possessio* could not be claimed, after a limited time.

8. The administration of the goods of an intestate, granted by the ordinary to his next of kin, in England, is not unlike the possession of goods, granted by the Roman prætor.

CHAPTER XII.

OF THE ACQUISITION OF PROPERTY BY ARROGATION; AND OTHER CIVIL MODES OF ACQUIRING, MENTIONED IN THE INSTITUTIONS.

Inst. Lib. III. Tit. 11, 12, 13.
Heinecc. *A. R.* Lib. III. Tit. 11, 12, 13. Tit. 30. § 2—8.
——— *El. J. C.* Lib. III. Tit. 11, 12, 13.
Taylor de Debitore in partes dissecando.
Blackstone's *Comm.* B. II. ch. 18. 31.

1. Besides the civil modes of acquiring property already explained, prescription, donation, succession; there are four others mentioned in the Institutions. I. ***Arrogatio.*** II. ***Bonorum addictio, libertatum servandarum causa.*** III. ***Sectio Bonorum.*** IV. ***Ex scto Claudiano.***

2. I. He who passed into another family by that species of adoption, called arrogation, transferred himself, and all his rights, except such as perished by the change of family, to the arrogator. This was the acquisition of property by arrogation.

3. II. If a testator in his last will had given freedom to slaves, and the testament afterwards became *destitute;* the slaves lost their freedom. To prevent this, the effects of the deceased were by the prætor *addicted*, or made over, to one or more of the manumitted slaves, or to any other person, who was admitted a testamentary heir, giving caution to pay the creditors; and by this means the slaves

obtained their freedom. This mode of acquiring property was called *bonorum addictio, libertatum servandarum causa.*

4. III. The effects of debtors, in case of insolvency, were assigned by the prætor to a certain person, in order to be *sold* and divided among the several creditors. This was the mode of acquiring property *per sectionem bonorum.*

5. The history of the Roman Law, with regard to debtors; and the Decemviral Law, which consigned the debtor into the hands of his creditors, with liberty to *cut the body* into pieces for their respective debts; explained.

6. The assignment of the effects of debtors, as practised by the old Civil Law, gave place to the law of *cession,* introduced by the Christian Emperors; by which debtors were obliged to surrender all their goods to their creditors upon oath.

7. The laws of bankruptcy and insolvency in England resemble the law of cession among the Romans.

8. IV. The mode of acquiring property *ex scto Claudiano*[1] was abolished by Justinian.

[1] See the History of this *Senâtus-consultum* in Tacit. Annal. L. XII. c. 53.

CHAPTER XIII.

OF OBLIGATIONS IN GENERAL.

Inst. Lib. III. Tit. 14.
Hoppii *Comm.* Lib. III. Tit. 14.
Heinecc. *A. R.* } Lib. III.
——— *El. J. C.* } Tit. 14.

Wood's *Inst. of the Civ. Law.* B. III. ch. 1.
Vinnii *Comm.* III. 14.
Pothier, *Obligations.*[1]

1. PROPERTY in action, when considered with regard to the person *from* whom it is due, is called obligation; when considered with regard to the person *to* whom it is due, it is called *Jus ad Rem.*

2. Obligation is a bond of law or equity, and sometimes of both, by which a person is laid under a necessity to give or to do something.

3. Obligations were, 1. Natural: which were, (1) Perfect. (2) Imperfect. 3. Civil. 4. Mixt. Mixt obligations were, 1. Civil. 2. Prætorian.

4. Obligations might arise from a lawful or unlawful act: the former sort were called *contractus;* the latter *delicta.*

5. When the agreement in a contract was not expressed, but presumed, it was called *quasi contractus.* When an unlawful act was committed through negligence, and not ill design, it was called *quasi delictum.*

6. From hence obligations were distributed into four species. I. *Ex contractu.* II. *Quasi ex contractu.* III. *Ex delicto.* IV. *Quasi ex delicto.*

[1] Pothier's Treatise on Obligations has been translated from the French into English by Sir W. D. Evans, with an Appendix and Notes illustrative of the English Law.

CHAPTER XIV.

OF OBLIGATIONS EX CONTRACTU, OR FROM CONTRACTS PROPERLY SO CALLED.

Hoppii *Comm.* Lib. III. Tit. 14.
Heinecc. *A. R.* } Lib. III. Tit. 14.
——— *El. J. C.* }
Wood's *Inst. of the Civ. Law.* B. III. ch. 1.
Vinnii *Comm.* III. 14.
Pothier, *Obligations.*
Blackstone's *Comm.* B. II. ch. 25. 30.
Jones, Sir W., *Bailments.*
Fonblanque's *Equity.* B. I. V. 1.

1. A CONTRACT, properly so called, is an agreement, upon sufficient consideration, to do, or not to do, a particular thing; with an obligation, at least on one side, and an action to enforce the performance.

2. Pacts and contracts were different from each other. *Pacta* were, 1. *Nuda.* 2. *Legitima.* 3. *Adjecta.*

3. Property in action may be transferred, in England, by a contract: but no contract is binding, by the English laws, unless attended with a consideration: which is, 1. A good. 2. A valuable consideration.

4. Contracts were, some of them, *bonæ fidei;* others *stricti juris.* In the former, equity and good faith were more considered than the bare words of the convention: in the latter, nothing could be demanded, but what had been expressly covenanted by the contracting parties.

5. In estimating the damage occasioned by either of the parties acceding to a contract, it was considered whether such damage were owing to a *dolus*, a *casus fortuitus*, or a *culpa*. *Culpa* was of three sorts; *lata, levis, levissima.*

6. In contracts of partial benefit, where the advantage was on the side of the giver, the receiver was answerable for a *dolus* and *culpa lata* only; where the advantage was on the side of the receiver, such receiver was answerable even for the *culpa levissima.* In contracts of mutual benefit, the parties, besides a *dolus* and *culpa lata,* were answerable for the *culpa levis,* but not the *levissima.*

7. Contracts were, I. Innominate. II. Nominate.

8. Innominate contracts were usually ranged under four classes, expressive of the consideration on which they were founded. 1. *Do ut des.* 2. *Do ut facias.* 3. *Facio ut des.* 4. *Facio ut facias.*

9. Nominate contracts were of four kinds, expressive of the ways in which they were formed. I. Real. II. Verbal. III. Literal. IV. Consensual.

CHAPTER XV.

OF REAL CONTRACTS.

Inst. Lib. III. Tit. 15.
Hoppii *Comm.* Lib. III. Tit. 15.
Heinecc. *A. R.* } Lib. III. Tit. 15.
——— *El. J. C.* }
Wood's *Inst. of the Civ. Law.* B. III. ch. 2.
Esprit des Loix. Liv. XXII. ch. 19. 22.
Voet Comm. ad Pand. Lib. XII. Tit. 1. § 24.
Grotius *de J. B. et P.* Lib. II. Cap. XII. § 20, 21.
Vinnii *Comm.* III. 15.
Rutherforth's *Inst. of Nat. Law.* Vol. I. ch. 13.
Blackstone's *Comm.* B. II. ch. 10. 30.

1. REAL contracts were those, in which, besides the consent of the parties, the delivery of some thing was required, to perfect the obligation. These were four in number. I. *Mutuum.* II. *Commodatum.* III. *Depositum.* IV. *Pignus.*

2. I. *Mutuum* is a loan of consumable goods, called *res fungibiles*, lent on condition of a return in kind.

3. In a loan of money, it might happen that the value altered after the contract: whether in such a case the payment should be made according to the price the money bore at the time of the contract, or at the time of payment; considered.

4. A *mutuum* allowed of no recompence, by way of interest. When a loan of consumable goods carried interest with it, it was called *foenus.*

5. The regulations of the Roman law concerning interest for money; and the method of computing it; explained.

6. The highest rate of interest for common loans, permitted by the Roman law, before the age of Justinian, was *twelve per cent.:* this was called *usuræ asses,* and *usura centesima,* or *legitima.* Justinian reduced it to a *triens,* or *four per cent.*

7. The regulations of the law of England concerning interest.

8. The taking of interest for money is not unlawful.

9. II. *Commodatum* is a loan of inconsumable goods, lent gratuitously, for a certain use, on condition of having the same returned in *specie.*

10. III. *Depositum* is the delivery of a thing in trust to another, on condition of restoring it to the owner on demand. Such a contract, in the law of England, is called simple bailment.

11. *Depositum* was of two kinds. 1. *Simplex.* 2. *Miserabile.*

12. The nature of a *sequestrum,* and in what respects it differed from a *depositum;* explained.

13. IV. *Pignus* is the delivery of a thing to a creditor, as a security for money lent, on condition of returning it to the owner after payment of the debt.

14. When the thing pledged was not delivered to the creditor, but continued in possession of the debtor, the contract was called *hypotheca.*

15. In England, a moveable chattel, delivered as security for money lent, is called a pawn. Estates in land, granted for the like purpose, are called estates *in vadio,* or in gage; being, 1. *in vivo vadio,* or living gage. 2. *In mortuo vadio,* or mort gage.

16. Pledges, by the Civil Law, were, 1. Express. 2. Tacit. They were also, 1. General, of a man's whole estate. 2. Particular, of some one thing only.

17. Sometimes the creditor had the profits of the pledge, by way of interest: this was called *pactum antichreseos.*

18. In case of delay of payment, the creditor had power to sell the pledge; allowing the debtor two years, after notice given, to redeem it[1].

19. In a mortgage in England, if the money be not paid at the day assigned, the property of the land becomes absolutely vested in the mortgagee, by the Common Law; but may be reclaimed by the right owner, by what is called the *equity of redemption:* and the same indulgence is allowed in a pawn of goods.

20. V. Besides the four real contracts now mentioned; there is a fifth, not treated of in the Institutions, called *precarium:* when one grants the use of some thing to another, at his request, till such time as the grantor shall recall it.

[1] Inst. II. Tit. 8. § 1.

CHAPTER XVI.

OF VERBAL CONTRACTS.

Inst. Lib. III. Tit. 16—21.
Hoppii *Comm.* Lib. III. Tit. 16—21.
Heinecc. *A. R.* Lib. III. Tit. 16—20. Tit. 21.
——— *El. J. C.* Lib. III. Tit. 16—21.
Wood's *Inst. of the Civ. Law.* B. III. ch. 3.
Vinnii *Comm.* III. 16—21.
Wood's *Inst. of the Laws of England.* B. II. ch. 3.
Blackstone's *Comm.* B. II. ch. 20.

1. VERBAL contracts were those, in which, besides the consent of the parties, a solemn form of words was required, to perfect the obligation. These were chiefly two. I. Stipulation. II. Fidejussion.

2. I. Stipulation is a contract, by which a person is bound to give or to do something, in consequence of a question asked, and a fit answer presently made to it.

3. Both the parties in a contract of stipulation were denominated *rei:* the person that asked the question, was called *reus stipulandi vel credendi;* he that returned the answer, *reus promittendi vel debendi.* When more stipulators or promisers than one were concerned, they were called *correi stipulandi,* or *correi promittendi.*

4. The promise in a stipulation might relate to something certain or uncertain. The stipulation itself might be, 1. Pure. 2. Conditional. 3. Performable on a certain day. 4. Or at a certain place.

5. Whatever was acquired by stipulation, the stipulator acquired for himself only, and not for any other: except he were, 1. A son under power. 2. A slave.

6. Effects of stipulation by a slave, in the cases of a *servus publicus, communis, hæreditarius.*

7. Stipulations, in respect of their causes, were, 1. Voluntary, by consent of parties; otherwise called conventional. 2. Necessary, by order from a magistrate. Necessary stipulations were, 1. Judicial. 2. Prætorian. 3. Common.

8. Stipulations became ineffectual, 1. By incapacity in the persons contracting. 2. Incapacity in the things, which were the subject of the contract. 3. Defect in the form.

9. Stipulations, in England, differ nothing from common covenants, whether nude, or on sufficient consideration: and by the stipulator is generally meant the promiser, not he to whom the promise is made, as in the Roman Law.

10. II. Fidejussion is a contract, in which a person bound himself, as a surety or accessory, for another, by the way of stipulation, without discharging the obligation of the principal.

11. Fidejussors, or sureties, were allowed in contracts of every kind; and they might accede to natural as well as civil obligations: but no surety could be bound for a greater sum than was owing from the principal.

12. If there were more sureties than one, the creditor might sue which of them he pleased for the whole, without convening the principal debtor.

13. To relieve sureties in such circumstances, the law allowed them three advantages. 1. *Beneficium divisionis.* 2. *Ordinis sive excussionis.* 3. *Cedendarum actionum.*

14. All persons might be sureties for others, unless specially forbidden, who could stipulate for themselves. Women were expressly prohibited by the *sctum Velleianum.*

15. By the laws of England, two or more persons may bind themselves in an obligation, jointly, or jointly and severally: in the former case, the obligee must sue them jointly; in the latter, he may sue them jointly, or any one of them at his election: and one surety may compel another towards payment of the debt, for which they were jointly bound.

CHAPTER XVII.

OF LITERAL CONTRACTS.

Inst. Lib. III. Tit. 22.
Hoppii *Comm.* Lib. III. Tit. 22.
Vinnii *Comm.* Lib. III. Tit. 22.
—— *Selectæ Juris Questiones.* Lib. I. cap. 41.

Heinecc. *A. R.* } Lib. III. Tit. 22.
—— *El. J. C.* }
Wood's *Inst. of the Civ. Law.* B. III. ch. 4.
Blackstone's *Comm.* B. II. ch. 30.

1. LITERAL contracts were those, in which, besides the consent of the parties, a note in writing was required, to perfect the obligation.

2. Such contracts, in the old Roman Law, were nothing more than a species of *novation*[1]; by which the obligation of a former debt was destroyed, and a new one by writing substituted in its room.

3. A literal contract, in the later laws of the Romans, was that, by which a person, who had confessed in writing he had received money from another, and had not retracted such confession within two years, became bound for the money, though it had never been paid.

4. If the creditor brought his action before the end of two years, the debtor could elude the force of it by what was called *Exceptio non numeratæ pecuniæ:* and in this case, the proof of payment lay upon the creditor.

[1] See Ch. XX. of this Book, pr. 8.

5. Whether, after the end of two years, the debtor could use his privilege of an exception, on condition he took the proof of non-payment on himself; considered.

6. A contract of debt in England is, 1. A debt of record. 2. By specialty. 3. By simple contract. But no exception, that the money was never paid, is allowed to debtors, who have acknowledged their debts in writing, as was permitted by the Civil Law.

CHAPTER XVIII.

OF CONSENSUAL CONTRACTS.

Inst. Lib. III. Tit. 23—27.
Hoppii *Comm.* Lib. III. Tit. 23—27..
Heinecc. *A. R.* } Lib. III. Tit. ——— *El. J. C.* } 23—27.
Wood's *Inst. of the Civ. Law.* B. III. ch. 5.
Taylor's *El. of the Civ. Law.* art. *Property.* p. 479—496.

Grotius *de J. B. et P.* Lib. II. Cap. XII. § 3. 7—19. 24.
Vinnii *Comm.* III. 23—27.
Rutherforth's *Inst. of Nat. Law.* Vol. I. ch. 13.
Wood's *Inst. of the Laws of Eng.* B. II. ch. 1.
Blackstone's *Comm.* B. II. ch. 3. 6. 9. 12. 30.

1. CONSENSUAL contracts were those, in which the consent alone of the parties perfected the obligation. These were five in number. I. *Emptio venditio.* II. *Locatio conductio.* III. *Emphyteusis.* IV. *Societas.* V. *Mandatum.*

2. I. *Emptio venditio,* or buying and selling, is a contract, by which goods are delivered from one man to another, for a certain price.

3. The price of things is their comparative value. The inconveniencies of adjusting such value by the method of permutation or exchange occasioned the introduction of a common standard, called money.

4. An implied warranty was annexed to every sale, in respect to the title of the seller. Goods, sold without the owner's consent, were sometimes

taken from the buyer, and redelivered to the proprietor, by the sentence of the judge: such a judicial recovery of what another had acquired by a legal title was called Eviction.

5. In England, no contract for the sale of goods, worth ten pounds or upwards, is valid; except the buyer receives part of the goods, or gives something to the seller by way of earnest, or unless some note of the bargain in writing be signed by the parties, or their agents.

6. *Addictio in diem, pactum commissorium, jus retractus sive retrovendendi;* explained.

7. II. *Locatio conductio,* or letting and hiring, is a contract, by which the use of a thing, or the labour of a person, is granted by one man to another, for a certain time, in consideration of a certain rent.

8. If the hirer died before the expiration of his term, the remaining part was enjoyed by his heir.

9. III. *Emphyteusis* is a contract, by which lands or houses are given in perpetuity, or for a long term, on condition that the tenant shall improve the lands, and pay a yearly canon or quit-rent to the proprietor.

10. The emphyteutic contract was, 1. Civil. 2. Ecclesiastical.

11. Fee-farm rents, and copyhold estates in England, are similar to the emphyteutic contract of the Roman law.

12. IV. *Societas,* or partnership, is a contract, by which the goods or labour of two or more are united in a common stock, for the sake of sharing in the gain.

13. The gain and loss of the partners were adjusted, according to the value of what each had contributed: and the same proportions were observed in both.

14. The renunciation of any one of the partners, though without the consent of the others, put an end to the partnership.

15. Partnership, in the laws of England, is chiefly considered with respect to lands, and other estates, which are held by a plurality of tenants. Such estates are, 1. In joint-tenancy. 2. In coparcenary. 3. In common,

16. V. *Mandatum*, or a commission, is a contract, by which a lawful business is committed to the management of another, and by him undertaken to be performed, without pay or reward.

17. A commission might be constituted for the benefit, 1. Of the mandator. 2. Of the mandator and mandatee. 3. Of a third person. 4. Of a third person and the mandator. 5. Of a third person and the mandatee.

18. A commission for the sole benefit of the mandatee was of no force.

19. In the laws of England, the contract of *mandatum* is of no use.

CHAPTER XIX.

OF OBLIGATIONS QUASI EX CONTRACTU, OR FROM IMPROPER CONTRACTS.

Inst. Lib. III. Tit. 28, 29.	Wood's *Institute of the Civil Law.* B. III. ch. 6.
Hoppii *Comm.* Lib. III. Tit. 28, 29.	Vinnii *Comm.* III. 28, 29.
Heinecc. *A. R.* / ——— *El. J. C.* } Lib. III. Tit. 28, 29.	Blackstone's *Comm.* B. II. ch. 30. B. III. ch. 9.

1. IMPROPER or *quasi* contracts were those, in which the obligation was founded on the consent of the parties, not expressed, but presumed. These were six in number. I. *Negotiorum gestio.* II. *Tutela.* III. *Rei communis, vel* IV. *Hæreditatis administratio.* V. *Hæreditatis aditio.* VI. *Indebiti solutio.*

2. *Negotiorum gestio*, or a contract for business done, was that, by which one, who, without commission, had undertaken the management of the business of an absent person, and he, whose business was so undertaken, were reciprocally bound to each other: the one, to execute the business with fidelity and diligence; the other, to reimburse the expenses incident to the prosecution of it.

3. *Tutela* was a contract between tutor and pupil; by which the former was bound to administer faithfully the affairs of his pupil, and the latter to indemnify the tutor for all expenses incurred in the due execution of his office.

4. *Rei communis administratio* was a contract between two or more persons, to whom the same thing had been given, or left by way of legacy; by which each was bound to divide the thing so possessed in common, and to allow for all extraordinary costs in the care or keeping of it.

5. *Hæreditatis administratio* was a contract between co-heirs to the same estate; by which each was bound to divide the inheritance, and to settle all accounts relating to it, in a fair proportion.

6. *Hæreditatis aditio* was a contract, by which an heir, accepting the inheritance, was bound to the legatees, to pay them the legacies left by the testator.

7. *Indebiti solutio* was a contract, by which he, who, by mistake, had been paid what was not due to him, was bound to make restitution to the person who had paid him.

8. In some cases, this necessity of restitution was remitted.

9. Implied contracts are not unknown in the laws of England.

10. Obligations, whether arising from proper or improper contracts, might be acquired immediately, by a man's self: or mediately, by others, whom he had under power; as a son and a slave.

CHAPTER XX.

OF THE WAYS BY WHICH OBLIGATIONS, ARISING FROM PROPER AND IMPROPER CONTRACTS, WERE DISSOLVED.

Inst. Lib. III. Tit. 30. IV. 6. 30.
Hoppii *Comm.* Lib. III. Tit. 30.
Heinecc. *A. R.* Lib. III. Tit. 30. pr. § 1. 9—16.
—— *El. J. C.* Lib. III. Tit. 30.
Wood's *Inst. of the Civ. Law.* B. III. ch. 9.
Vinnii *Comm.* III. 30. and IV. 6. 30.
Blackstone's *Comm.* B. III. ch. 20.

1. OBLIGATIONS, arising from proper and improper contracts, were dissolved, 1. By the help of an exceptive plea. 2. By the operation of law.

2. The ways, by which obligations were dissolved by the operation of law, were, I. Common to all contracts. II. Peculiar to some exclusive of others.

3. I. The ways of dissolving an obligation, common to all contracts, were five. 1. Solution. 2. Compensation. 3. Confusion. 4. Oblation. 5. Novation.

4. Solution is, when a debtor, or some other in his name, makes an actual satisfaction to the proper creditor, by the payment of what is due.

5. Compensation, or stoppage, is a reckoning between debtor and creditor, by which the debtor *sets off* what is due to him from the creditor, in order to lessen or extinguish his debt.

6. Confusion is, when the obligation of the debtor and right of the creditor are united in the same person.

7. Oblation is a tender of the debt in money to the creditor; which money, if refused without cause, was afterwards sealed up, and deposited with the magistrate. This was called *Oblatio et consignatio*.

8. Novation is the change of the former obligation into another of the same or a different kind. This might be, 1. By a change of the persons; which was called delegation. 2. By a change in the obligation, the persons continuing the same.

9. Novations were, 1. Voluntary, by agreement of the parties. 2. Necessary, by contestation of suit.

10. II. The ways of dissolving an obligation, peculiar to some contracts, exclusive of others, were two. 1. Acceptilation. 2. Mutual consent.

11. Acceptilation is an imaginary payment, when a creditor acknowledges he has been paid a debt he has not actually received, with an intention to discharge his debtor.

12. Acceptilation was peculiar to verbal obligations, contracted by the way of stipulation. The form of a general discharge, invented by *Gallus Aquilius*, and called *Stipulatio Aquiliana*, by which obligations of all kinds were first reduced to verbal, and then dissolved by acceptilation[1]; explained.

[1] The form was this: Mævius, the creditor, first of all proposed a question to Titius, his debtor: *Quicquid te mihi, ex quacunque causa, dare facere oportet, oportebit; præsens, in diemve, aut sub conditione; quarumque rerum mihi tecum actio est, quæque vel adversus te petitio, vel adversus te persecutio est, eritve; quod-*

que

13. Mutual consent is, when all the parties, by agreement, recede from an obligation, not yet completed. This was peculiar to the contracts, called consensual.

que tu meum habes, tenes, possides; dolove malo fecisti, quo minus possideas: quanti quæque earum rerum res erit, tantam pecuniam tu mihi dare spondes? To which the answer, returned by Titius, was, *spondeo.* After this, Titius, the debtor proposed a question to Mævius, his creditor, thus: *Quod tibi jam me daturum spospondi, id habesne a me acceptum?* To which if the answer by Mævius was, *Habeo a te acceptum;* every obligation, of whatever kind, was dissolved, and Titius, the debtor, was entirely discharged.

CHAPTER XXI.

OF OBLIGATIONS EX DELICTO, OR FROM OFFENCES PROPERLY SO CALLED.

Inst. Lib. IV. Tit. 1. pr.
Heinecc. *A. R.* } Lib. IV. Tit. 1.
——— *El. J. C.* }
Wood's *Inst. of the Civ. Law.* B. III. ch. 7.
Esprit des Loix. Liv. VI. ch. 9—20.
Grotius *de J. B. et P.* Lib. II. cap. XVII. § 1—11. cap. XX. § 1—9. § 28—37.
Rutherforth's *Inst. of Nat. Law.* Vol. I. ch. 17, 18.
Blackstone's *Comm.* B. IV. ch. 1, 2, 3.
Principles of Penal Law. Ch. 2. 11.

1. In contracts, the obligation of the parties is voluntary: in offences, the law obliges them, whether they will or no.

2. Offences are acts, wilfully committed in violation of law.

3. Offences, as doing damage, oblige the offender to make reparation: as indicating a vicious will, they render him liable to suffer punishment.

4. Punishment is an evil suffered for an evil done.

5. The end of punishment is to prevent future offences.

6. All persons are capable of committing offences, and liable to the punishments appropriated to them, who labour under no defect of will.

7. Offences are, 1. Private. 2. Public.

8. Private offences, called in the Roman Law *maleficia* or *delicta*, and in the laws of England civil injuries, are a violation of the rights due to individuals.

9. Public offences are a violation of the rights due to the community: these are considered under the third general division of the objects of the Civil Law, which treats of actions[1].

10. The prosecution of private offences, by the Roman Law was, 1. Civil. 2. Criminal.

11. The Civil prosecution of private offences was, in order to redress an injury, as it affected an individual. This redress was obtained, 1. By reparation of the damage done. 2. By the punishment of the offender. 3. By both.

12. The criminal prosecution of private offences was, in order to punish a crime, as it affected the community. This was done, 1. By corporal punishment. 2. By a pecuniary fine, payable to the Exchequer.

13. *Delicta*, or private offences, properly so called, were in number four. I. *Furtum*. II. *Rapina*. III. *Damnum*. IV. *Injuria*.

[1] See Book III. Ch. XII.

CHAPTER XXII.

OF FURTUM, OR THEFT.

Inst. Lib. IV. Tit. 1.
Hoppii *Comm.* Lib. IV. Tit. 1.
Heinecc. *A. R.* / ——— *El. J. C.* } Lib. IV. Tit. 1.
Wood's *Inst. of the Civ. Law.* B. III. ch. 7.
Esprit des Loix. Liv. XXIX. ch. 12, 13.

Grotius *de J. B. et P.* Lib. II. ch. I. § 12, 13.
Rutherforth's *Inst. of Nat. Law.* Vol. I. ch. 16.
Wood's *Inst. of the Laws of England.* B. III. ch. 1.
Blackstone's *Comm.* B. IV. ch. 16, 17.
Principles of Penal Law. Ch. 22.

1. FURTUM, or theft, is the fraudulent taking, and carrying away, of the moveable goods of another, for the sake of gain.

2. Theft might be committed, not only by subtraction of the thing itself, belonging to another, but also by taking away the use or the possession of it.

3. Theft could not regularly be committed in such things as had no owner.

4. *Furtum,* by the old Roman Law, was divided into four kinds. 1. *Conceptum.* 2. *Oblatum.* 3. *Prohibitum.* 4. *Non exhibitum*[1].

[1] *Furtum,* in the Latin language, is used, either to signify the act of theft, or *res furtiva,* the thing stolen. In this latter sense it is to be understood, when joined by the Roman lawyers with the words *conceptum, oblatum, prohibitum, non exhibitum.*

5. *Conceptum* was, when the thing stolen was searched for, and found upon the thief before witnesses. The ancient method of enquiring after things stolen, *per lancem et licium;* explained.

6. *Oblatum* was, when the thing stolen was found upon one, who had received it from the thief, not knowing it to have been stolen.

7. *Prohibitum* was, when one was hindered from enquiring after a thing stolen, in the presence of witnesses.

8. *Non exhibitum* was, when one refused to exhibit a thing stolen, that had been searched for, and found in his possession.

9. Theft, by the later law of the Romans, was 1. Manifest. 2. Not manifest.

10. Manifest theft was, when the thief was taken in the fact: or apprehended, with the goods upon him, before he had carried them to the place, where they were to remain that night. A thief, so apprehended in England, is said to be taken *with the maner*, or *in flagranti delicto.*

11. Not manifest theft was, when the thief was not taken in the fact, but after he had carried the goods to the place designed.

12. Theft was further distinguished into diurnal and nocturnal. The latter answers to what is called, in the law of England, burglary; or the breaking and entering, by night, into a dwelling-house, with intent to commit a felony: or the entering of a dwelling-house of another, with intent to commit felony; or being in such dwelling-house, and the committing of any felony; and in either case, the breaking out[1]

[1] See 7 and 8 George IV. c. 29. § 11.

of such dwelling-house in the night-time. The punishment is death.

13. Larceny, or theft, by the law of England, is the felonious taking and carrying away, of the personal goods of another: and is, 1. Simple. 2. Mixt.

14. Simple larceny is the felonious taking, and carrying away, of the personal goods of another; but neither from the house, nor the person, of the owner, nor by night.

15. The distinction between grand and petit larceny is now abolished[2].

16. Mixt larceny is the felonious taking, and carrying away, of the personal goods of another, 1. From the house. 2. From the person.

17. In a Civil prosecution of theft, the party injured might sue, 1. For the restitution of the thing stolen. 2. For the punishment of the thief: which punishment was a forfeiture of four times the value, when the theft was manifest; or of double the value, when the theft was not manifest. 3. For both.

18. In a criminal prosecution of theft, the punishment was different at different times; but was never death, except in the case of a slave, till the age of the later emperors.

19. The prosecution of theft was allowed, not only to the owner of the thing stolen, but to any other person, who had an interest in its safety.

[2] See 7 and 8 George IV. c. 29. § 2.

CHAPTER XXIII.

OF RAPINA, OR ROBBERY.

Inst. Lib. IV. Tit. 2.
Hoppii *Comm.* Lib. IV. Tit. 2.
Heinecc. *A. R.* } Lib. IV. Tit. 2.
——— *El. J. C* } Lib. IV. Tit. 2.
Wood's *Inst. of the Civ. Law.* B. III. ch. 7.

Wood's *Inst. of the Laws of Eng.* B. III. ch. 1.
Blackstone's *Comm.* B. IV. ch. 17.
Principles of Penal Law. Ch. 22.

1. RAPINA, or robbery, is the violent taking, from the person of another, of money or goods, for the sake of gain.

2. Rapine, or robbery from the person, related to such goods as were moveable: when immoveable goods were violently taken from the possessor, the offence was called Invasion.

3. A man was not permitted to take by violence from another, even what he had reason to believe his own.

4. In a Civil prosecution of robbery, the punishment was a forfeiture of four times the value, if the offence was prosecuted within the year; or of the simple value, if prosecuted after the year. But in the forfeiture of four times the value, the restitution of the thing itself was included.

5. The criminal prosecution was appropriated to such robberies as were of the more desperate

kind; and the punishments were different, according to the circumstances of the fact.

6. The prosecution of robbery was allowed, not only to the owner of the goods taken by the robber, but to any other person, who had an interest in their safety.

7. In England, that species of mixt larceny, which is called larceny from the person, is subdivided into two kinds. 1. Private stealing, which is punished with transportation or imprisonment. 2. Robbery; or the felonious and violent taking, from the person of another, of any chattel, money, or valuable security, putting him in fear. The punishment is death[1].

[1] See 7 and 8 George IV. c. 27, and 7 and 8 George IV. c. 29. § 6.

CHAPTER XXIV.

OF DAMNUM, OR DAMAGE.

Inst. Lib. IV. Tit. 3.
Hoppii *Comm.* Lib. IV. Tit. 3.
Heinecc. *A. R.* } Lib. IV. Tit. 3.
——— *El. J. C.* }
Wood's *Inst. of the Civ. Law.* B. III. ch. 7.
Wood's *Inst. of the Laws of England.* B. I. ch. 6.
Blackstone's *Comm.* B. III. ch. 8. 12. B. IV. ch. 14, 15.

1. DAMNUM, or damage, is the loss or diminution of what is a man's own, occasioned by the fraud or fault of a free man.

2. The redress of damages was the object of the Aquilian Law.

3. The Aquilian Law consisted of three parts. In the first it was provided, That he who killed a slave belonging to another, or such of his beasts as went under the denomination of cattle, should forfeit to the owner the highest price, such slave or beast might have been sold for, at any time within a year before the wound was given.

4. When a slave or beast was slain by accident, or in the way of self-defence; the slayer was not subjected to the penalty of the Aquilian Law. The killing of a human creature, in such circum-

stances, is called, in the laws of England, excusable homicide.

5. In the case of a slave, slain maliciously, the slayer, besides being liable to be sued for damages, was also obnoxious to capital punishment, as guilty of a public crime. In England, a person, after being prosecuted criminally for felony and acquitted, may be sued in a Civil action for damages, at the instance of the injured party.

6. The second part of the Aquilian Law is lost; but probably related to the case of corrupting a slave belonging to another, for which it prescribed a penalty.

7. In the third part of the Aquilian Law it was provided, That he who wounded the slave or cattle of another; or killed, wounded, or hurt any other part of his property, animate, or inanimate; should forfeit to the owner the highest price, the beast or goods might have been sold for, at any time within thirty days before the damage was done.

8. A freeman, that was wounded, had no *direct* remedy from this part of the Aquilian Law; Yet, by an equitable interpretation, such a one could sue for the loss of his time, and the expense of his cure.

9. In England the malicious killing, or maiming, of a human[1] creature is punished with death. The malicious killing, maiming, or wounding, of cattle[2] is a felony punishable with transportation or

[1] See 9 George IV. c. 31. § 11, 12.

[2] See 7 and 8 George IV. c. 30. § 16.

imprisonment. The beating, confining, or disabling of a man's servant is an injury which is remedied by action on the case.

10. The Aquilian Law, now explained, related to the case of damage *done;* called *Damnum datum.* Damage was further considered, 1. As *doing.* 2. As *not yet done.* The redress of the former was had from the prohibition of the prætor, called *Nuntiatio novi operis;* of the latter, from what was called *Cautio de damno infecto.*

CHAPTER XXV.

OF INJURIA, OR INJURY.

Inst. Lib. IV. Tit. 4.
Hoppii *Comm.* Lib. IV. Tit. 4.
Heinecc. *A. R.* } Lib. IV. Tit. 4.
——— *El. J. C.* }
Wood's *Inst. of the Civ. Law.* B. III. ch. 7.
Esprit des Loix. Liv. IV. ch. 15. 19.
Wood's *Inst. of the Laws of England.* B. III. ch. 3.
Blackstone's *Comm.* B. III. ch. 8. B. IV. ch. 11.

1. INJURIA, or injury, is any thing maliciously done or said, by which another is hurt in his body or reputation.

2. Injuries were, I. Real. II. Verbal: and both were divided into, 1. Simple. 2. Atrocious.

3. Real injuries were those, in which an unlawful act was done.

4. Verbal injuries were those, in which slanderous and malicious words were spoken.

5. Under verbal injuries were included libels[1]: or malicious defamations of another, in writing, or

[1] A libel, in the Roman Law, is called *Famosus libellus;* and, by a constitution of the Emperors Valentinian and Valens, the finder and publisher of a libel was equally obnoxious to punishment as the author. *Si quis Famosum Libellum sive domi, sive in publico vel quocunque loco, ignarus repererit; aut corrumpat priusquam alter inveniat, aut nulli confiteatur inventum. Si vero non statim easdem chartulas vel corruperit, vel igni consumpserit,* *sed*

otherwise, tending to diminish his good name and reputation.

6. In what cases the truth of defamatory words, spoken or written, would serve to excuse the defamer; explained.

7. Injuries might be committed against a man's own person, or against those who were under his protection. An injury done to a slave was an injury to his master.

8. The redress of injuries was had from the Decemviral Law, the Law of the Prætor, and the *Lex Cornelia.*

9. By the Decemviral Law, the punishment of a real injury, in the case of a broken limb, was retaliation; of a verbal injury, of the atrocious sort, the punishment was death. Injuries of a lighter kind, real or verbal, were punished by a pecuniary fine.

10. The Law of the Prætor allowed the party injured to estimate the damage received; which the judge might follow, or lessen, at discretion.

11. The *Lex Cornelia* related to real injuries offered to the body, such as in England are called Battery; and to the entry into the house of another by force: for which the party injured had a recompense in damages.

sed vim earum manifestaverit; sciat se, tanquam auctorem hujusmodi delicti, capitali sententiæ subjugandum. C. 9. 36. It is curious to observe, how closely this constitution is copied in the Statutes of the University of Cambridge. *Qui Famosum Libellum, sive domi sive foras, ignarus repererit; aut corrumpat, aut igni tradat, antequam alter inveniat. Qui vero alteri fateatur inventum, et vim illius declaraverit; sciat se tanquam auctorem delicti, puniendum, et Universitate expellatur.* Stat. Eliz. C. XLVII. *De modestia et morum urbanitate.*

12. The injurious party, besides a civil, was liable to a criminal prosecution, both by the Prætorian and Cornelian Laws.

13. In a criminal prosecution, the punishment for atrocious injuries was death, or banishment: for injuries, of a less heinous sort, the offender was rendered incapable of being a witness, or of making a testament.

14. Injuries to the body or reputation may be prosecuted in England, 1. By action, at the suit of the party injured. 2. By indictment or information, at the suit of the crown. By the former method, the party injured has a recompense in damages: by the latter, the offender is subjected to a corporal punishment, or a pecuniary fine.

15. Injuries were abolished, 1. By death; whether of the injurious, or the injured party. 2. Remission. 3. Satisfaction. 4. Prescription.

CHAPTER XXVI.

OF OBLIGATIONS QUASI EX DELICTO, OR FROM IMPROPER OFFENCES.

Inst. Lib. IV. Tit. 5.
Hoppii *Comm.* Lib. IV. Tit. 5.
Heinecc. *A. R.* / ——— *El. J. C.* } Lib. IV. Tit. 5.
Wood's *Inst. of the Civ. Law.* B. III. ch. 8.
Blackstone's *Comm.* B. III. ch. 9. 25.

1. IMPROPER offences, or *quasi delicta*, were those, in which an unlawful act was committed through negligence, without ill design. These were four in number, I. An erroneous sentence given by a judge. II. Things thrown or poured from a house. III. Things hung or placed so as to be dangerous to those who passed under. IV. Things damaged or stolen in a ship or inn.

2. I. If a judge, through ignorance of the law, pronounced an erroneous sentence; he *made the suit his own*, and became liable to pay the damage which such sentence had occasioned.

3. II. When things were thrown or poured from a house, without design, by which passengers were hurt or incommoded; the inhabitant of that house, whether proprietor or tenant, was compellable to make reparation for the damage done.

4. III. When things were hung or placed in any such way, as to be dangerous to those who passed under them; the owner was punishable by fine, whether any one were hurt by their fall or not.

5. IV. When things were damaged qr stolen by any of the servants belonging to a ship or inn; the master of such ship or inn was liable to pay the double value. When the damage or theft was done by a stranger or persons unknown, the master was simply obliged to make good the loss.

6. In all cases, in which an injury results from negligence or a want of proper caution, compensation is awarded by the laws of England to the party injured, and occasionally punishments are imposed.

BOOK III.

OF ACTIONS.

CHAPTER I.

OF ACTIONS IN GENERAL, AND THEIR SEVERAL KINDS.

Inst. Lib. IV. Tit. 6.
Hoppii *Comm.* Lib. IV. Tit. 6.
Heinecc. *A. R.* Lib. IV. Tit. 6. § 23—38.
——— *El. J. C.* Lib. IV. Tit. 6.
Wood's *Inst. of the Civ. Law.* B. IV. ch. 1. 3.
Wood's *Inst. of the Laws of England.* B. IV. ch. 4.
Blackstone's *Comm.* B. III. ch. 1. 8, 9, 10, 11.

1. In case of privation or infringement of a man's rights, the law of nature and of each particular society entitles the injured party to redress.

2. The means, or instruments, by which redress is principally to be obtained, are civil suits, or actions, in a Court of Justice.

3. Actions are the legal demand of a man's right; or the means, which the law puts into his hands of pursuing and recovering those rights, whether perfect or imperfect, of which he is unjustly deprived.

4. Actions, in the Roman Law, with respect to their origin, were, 1. Civil. 2. Prætorian. With respect to their subject, they were distinguished into 1. Real. 2. Personal. 3. Mixt.

5. Real actions, otherwise called vindications, were those, in which a man demanded some certain thing that was *his own;* and were founded on dominion, or *jus in re.* Personal actions, denominated also condictions, were those, in which a man demanded what was barely *due* to him; and were founded on obligation, or *jus ad rem.* Mixt actions were those, in which some specific thing was demanded, and also some personal obligations were claimed to be performed.

6. Real actions were, 1. *Rei vindicatio,* properly so called. 2. *Actio confessoria.* 3. *Negatoria.* 4. *Publiciana.* 5. *Rescissoria.* 6. *Pauliana.* 7. *Serviana.* 8. *Quasi-serviana.* 9. *Actiones præjudiciales.*

7. *Rei vindicatio* was granted to the owner of a certain corporeal thing, in order to have it restored by the person in possession. To this action, which determined the right of property, another was previously necessary, called *Lis vindiciarum,* in order to determine the right of possession, during the time of suit[1].

[1] See the oration of Cicero *pro Muræna,* c. 11, 12. where the form of claiming the possession of an immoveable is preserved. In the story of Appius and Virginia, related by Livy, in his third book, the great aggravation of the injury, there complained of, consisted in this; that Appius assigned Virginia to Claudius, who claimed her as his *ancilla;* or decreed the *Vindiciæ,* (that is, the *possession* of Virginia, till such time as her state, whether of freedom or slavery, could be tried,) *secundum servitutem,* in favour of slavery; instead of *secundum libertatem,* in favour of liberty; as the law required. *Appius, amore ardens,—M. Claudio clienti negotium dedit, ut Virginem in servitutem assereret, neque cederet secundum libertatem postulantibus Vindicias.—Ad tribunal Appii perventum est. Notam judici fabulam petitor, quippe apud ipsum auctorem argumenti, peragit, puellam,*

8. Actio *confessoria, et negatoria,* related to incorporeal things, or services. By the former, one *claimed* a service, real or personal, in an estate belonging to another: by the latter, the owner of a particular estate *denied* that such estate was obnoxious to a service.

9. Actio *publiciana* was instituted by one, who had lost a thing, of which he had *bona fide* obtained the possession: in order to have it restored, under colour that he had acquired a property in it by prescription.

10. Actio *rescissoria* was instituted by one, who on account of absence had lost his right of property in a thing, which another had acquired by the title of prescription; in order to have it restored, under colour that no such prescription had taken place.

11. Actio *pauliana* was granted to creditors, for the recovery of goods, fraudulently alienated by their debtors.

12. Actio *serviana* was granted to the letter of a rural estate, for the recovery of goods, obligated by the hirer as a security for his rent.

13. Actio *quasi-serviana* was granted to creditors, to obtain possession of goods, pledged or hypothecated by their debtors.

14. Actiones *præjudiciales* (so called because they were to be *first* decided before the principal

puellam domi suæ natam, furtoque inde in domum Virginii translatam; id se—probaturum:—interim dominum sequi ancillam, æquum esse. Advocati puellæ postulant, ut rem integram in patris adventum differat; lege ab ipso lata vindicias det secundum libertatem.

action could be brought) were those instituted concerning a man's civil state or condition. These were three in number. 1. *De libertate.* 2. *De ingenuitate.* (Both called *Actiones ex causa liberali.*) 3. *De partu agnoscendo.*

15. Personal actions arose, 1. From law. 2. From equity. 3. From contracts. 4. From offences.

16. Personal actions arising from *law*, called *condictiones ex lege*, had place, when an obligation had been introduced by a new *law*, and no particular action had been expressed, by which that obligation might be enforced.

17. Of this sort were the condictitious actions, granted to *rei*, or defendants, *contra actores plus petentes*, against actors, or plaintiffs, who had inserted in their libels a greater sum than was due: and *contra viatores sive executores litium*, against the officers of a Court of Justice, who had been guilty of exaction, contrary to law.

18. Of personal actions arising from equity, the principal were, 1. *Actio ad exhibendum*, to compel the possessors of moveable goods to exhibit them to the persons interested in having them produced. 2. *Restitutiones in integrum*, to rescind the contracts of minors, and such as had been made through fear or fraud.

19. Personal actions, arising from contracts, were of various kinds; corresponding to the several species of contracts, proper and improper, explained in the second book.

20. Proper contracts were, 1. Innominate; to each of which was appropriated a general action on the case, called *actio in factum*, or *præscriptis ver-*

bis. 2. Nominate; which were, 1. Real. 2. Verbal. 3. Literal. 4. Consensual.

21. Real contracts were, 1. *Mutuum*. 2. *Commodatum*. 3. *Depositum*. 4. *Pignus*. The actions belonging to which were, 1. *Condictio certi ex mutuo*. 2. *Actio commodati, directa et contraria*. 3. *Depositi, directa et contraria*. 4. *Pignoratitia, directa et contraria*.

22. Verbal contracts were, 1. *Stipulatio*. 2. *Fidejussio*. From these came, 1. *Actio certi ex stipulatu*, when the stipulation concerned a *res certa: incerti ex stipulatu*, when it concerned a *res incerta*. 2. *Beneficia divisionis, ordinis, cedendarum actionum*. From literal contracts came *condictio ex chirographo*.

23. Consensual contracts were, 1. *Emptio venditio*. 2. *Locatio conductio*. 3. *Emphyteusis*. 4. *Societas*. 5. *Mandatum*. The actions belonging to which were, 1. *Empti; venditi: redhibitoria: quanti minoris*. 2. *Locati; conducti*. 3. *Emphyteuticaria: directa et contraria*. 4. *Pro socio*. 5. *Mandati, directa et contraria*.

24. Improper contracts were, 1. *Negotiorum gestio*. 2. *Tutela*. 3. *Rei communis administratio*. 4. *Hæreditatis administratio*. 5. *Hæreditatis aditio*. 6. *Indebiti solutio*. To these belonged the actions, 1. *Negotiorum gestorum, directa et contraria*. 2. *Tutelæ, directa et contraria*. 3. *Communi dividundo*. 4. *Familiæ erciscundæ*. 5. *Ex testamento*. 6. *Condictio indebiti*.

25. To personal actions, arising from improper contracts, may be referred, 1. *Actio de constituta pecunia;* for the payment of money *constituted*, or promised, without any preceding stipulation. 2. *De peculio;* when one had contracted with the son or slave of another, to compel the father or master to perform the contract, as far as the *peculium* of each would extend. 3. *De jurejurando voluntario;* when one, at the instance of the adverse party, had sworn that a debt was really due to him, to compel the adversary to the payment of it.

26. Personal actions, arising from *offences*, corresponded to the several species of offences, proper and improper, explained in the second book.

27. Proper offences were, 1. *Furtum.* 2. *Rapina.* 3. *Damnum.* 4. *Injuria.* To these belonged, 1. *Actio furti: condictio furtiva.* 2. *De vi bonorum raptorum;* or *actio furti.* 3. *Ex lege Aquilia.* 4. *Injuriarum; decemviralis, prætoria ex lege Cornelia.*

28. To personal actions, arising from proper offences, may be referred, 1. *Actio de albo corrupto;* against him, who had defaced or damaged the tablet, on which the prætor proposed his edict. 2. *De in jus vocando;* against a son or *libertus,* who had commenced a suit against a parent or patron, without leave from the prætor. 3. *De in jus vocato non eximendo;* against those, who had prevented a person's appearance to a process in a Court of Justice, on the day agreed on. 4. *De servo corrupto;* against him, who had corrupted the morals of a slave. 5. *De calumniatoribus:* on account of money given to move, or not to move, a suit against another; to compel the receiver to make restitution.

29. From improper offences arose a general action on the case, called *Actio in factum,* or *præscriptis verbis.*

30. Mixt actions were, 1. *Hæreditatis petitio;* instituted by an heir, in order to have the inheritance

restored by the persons in possession. 2. The three actions called ***Judicia Divisoria:*** viz. ***Communi Dividundo: Familiæ Erciscundæ:*** (both also reckoned among actions merely personal) and ***Finium Regundorum,*** instituted to settle the bounds of contiguous rural estates.

31. Actions were persecutory, 1. Of the thing. 2. Of the penalty. 3. Of both.

32. Actions might be laid for the recovery of the simple, double, triple, or quadruple value, of the loss sustained: beyond which no penal action could extend.

33. Actions were, 1. ***Bonæ fidei;*** in which the judge, appointed by the prætor, was allowed to estimate what was due from the litigant parties, according to equity and good faith. 2. ***Stricti juris;*** in which the judge was restrained to the express words of convention between the parties. 3. ***Arbitrary;*** in which the ***reus,*** refusing to make the satisfaction required, was condemned at the arbitration of the judge.

34. To actions ***bonæ fidei*** belonged, 1. ***Actio ex stipulatu de dote repetenda;*** granted to the wife for the recovery of her ***dos.*** 2. ***De estimato;*** granted to him who had delivered to another a thing, ***estimated*** at a certain price, on purpose that it might be sold; to have the thing restored, or the price paid. 3. ***Ex permutatione;*** granted to him, who had delivered a thing to another, by way of ***exchange;*** to have the thing promised in return, or its value: with many other actions besides.

35. An example of an ***arbitrary*** action was that ***de eo quod certo loco:*** when a thing, stipulated to be given or done at one certain place, was demanded by the actor at another; the judge allowing for the loss incurred by the *reus*, in performing his engagements at a different place from that agreed on.

36. In some actions a certain thing was demanded; in others an uncertain: but in either case the actor was liable to a penalty, if he demanded *more* than his due. More than was due might be demanded four ways: *re, causa, loco, tempore.*

37. In some actions, an actor might sue for the *whole* of what was due to him; in others he was restrained to sue for *less* than the whole.

38. When an actor was restrained to sue for *less* than the whole, such restraint arose, 1. From the nature of the action itself. 2. From compensation or stoppage. 3. From a benefit, or privilege, indulged to particular persons: which was of two sorts; 1. *Beneficium competentiæ.* 2. *Beneficium cessionis.*

39. Actions were, 1. Direct, which descended from the express words of the law. 2. Useful, which descended from the meaning and interpretation of the law.

40. Sometimes the *reus* would institute an action, or cross-bill, against the actor, in the way of compensation or set-off: this was called *mutua petitio* or *reconventio.*

41. CUMULATIO was the junction of several actions depending on one and the same ground. Thus in the Court of Admiralty, seamen and others are permitted to join in the same suit, the general ground of action being the same.

42. In the laws of England civil[1] actions are, 1. Personal. 2. Mixt.

43. Personal actions are those which one man brings against another, 1. On account of a contract or debt for goods and chattels. 2. On account of an offence or trespass against his person or goods. 3. On account of an injury to or trespass on land.

44. Mixt actions are those, in which some real property is demanded, and also personal damages for the wrong sustained.

45. In actions the parties are called *plaintiff* and *defendant*.

46. In case of *ouster*, or dispossession of real property, whether by abatement, intrusion, or disseisin; the remedy to the legal owner, against the unlawful possessor, is, 1. By the mere entry of him, who hath the right. 2. By action.

47. The title to lands is tried by a writ of *ejectione firmæ;* where one, who hath the right, makes a lease to another of lands, for a term of years; and a third person enters and ousts the lessee; upon which the lessee brings an action of ejectment; by virtue of which the title of the lessor comes to be tried; and the lessee recovers, from the ejector or tenant, his term and damages.

48. In case of dispossession of personal property, the remedy to the plaintiff, or legal owner, against the defendant, or unlawful possessor, is restitution of the goods, taken or detained; with satisfaction in damages for the loss incurred. Which remedy is effected, 1. By action of replevin; or detinue. 2. Of trover and conversion.

[1] Real actions are abolished by 3 and 4 William IV. c. 27.

49. Personal property, when in action only, arises from contracts; which are, 1. Express. 2. Implied. Express contracts are, 1. Debts. 2. Covenants. 3. Promises or assumpsits. Implied contracts are such as arise from reason and justice, which the law *presumes* a man has undertaken to perform.

50. In case of violation of express contracts, the remedy is, 1. By action of debt. 2. Of covenant. 3. Of assumpsit. For non-performance of implied contracts, the remedy is by action on the case, grounded on the several *presumptive* assumpsits of the promiser.

CHAPTER II.

OF ACTIONS ARISING FROM THE CONTRACTS OF OTHERS; AND OF NOXAL ACTIONS.

Inst. Lib. IV. Tit. 7, 8, 9.
Hoppii *Comm.* Lib. III. Tit. 7, 8, 9.
Heinecc. *A. R.* } Lib. IV. Tit.
——— *El. J. C.* } 7, 8, 9.
Wood's *Inst. of the Civ. Law.* B. III. ch. 8.
Wood's *Inst. of the Laws of England.* B. II. ch. 2.
Blackstone's *Comm.* B. I. ch. 8. B. III. ch. 1. 12.

1. An action might arise from a contract, made either by the *reus* himself, or by others under his power; as a son or a slave.

2. Of this latter kind were the actions, 1. *Quod jussu.* 2. *Exercitoria.* 3. *Institoria.* 4. *Tributoria.* 5. *De in rem verso.* 6. *De peculio.*

3. *Quod jussu* was granted to those, who had contracted with a son or slave, by order of the father or master; to compel such father or master to stand to the agreement.

4. *Exercitoria* was granted to those, who had contracted with the master of a ship; to compel the owner or hirer of the ship to perform whatever was comprehended in the contract.

5. *Institoria* was granted to those, who had contracted with the factor of another; to compel the principal to performance.

6. *Tributoria* was granted to the creditors of a son or slave, engaged in trade with consent of the father or master; to compel such father or master to distribute the goods, or money arising from the goods, in proportion to the demands of each creditor.

7. *De in rem verso* was granted to those, who had contracted with a son or slave; in order to recover whatever the father or master, by means of such contract, had converted to their own advantage.

8. The action *de peculio* is explained in the preceding chapter[1].

9. No action was allowed for the recovery of money lent to a son under power, without consent of his father. This was ordered by the *Sctum Macedonianum.*

10. In case of an offence committed by a slave, and of damage done by a beast, the master of the slave and owner of the beast were liable to be convened, by what was called a noxal action.

11. The effect of such a noxal action was; that the master and owner had the alternative, either to pay for the damage done, or to deliver up the slave or beast to the actor.

12. Damage done by an irrational animal was called *pauperies;* and the action, descending from it, was called *actio de pauperie.*

13. In case of cattle straying and *feeding* in another's ground, the owner of the soil had an action *de pastu pecorum;* to compel the owner of the cattle either to pay for the damage done, or to give up his cattle. In England, cattle *damage feasant*

[1] See Prop. 25 of the preceding chapter.

may be *distrained* by the owner of the soil, and secured, or *pounded,* till satisfaction be made for the injury; and if not *redeemed,* may be *sold*[1] to pay the damage done, and the expense incurred in the keep of them.

14. In case of *hurt* received from an animal kept near a public road, an action on the case, *ex edicto Ædilitio,* lay against the owner of the animal for damages. In England, an animal, or thing inanimate, which is the occasion of death to a human creature, is forfeited, and becomes a Deodand.

[1] See 5 and 6 William IV. c. 59.

CHAPTER III.

OF THE PERSONS, BY AND AGAINST WHOM ACTIONS MIGHT BE BROUGHT; AND OF THE CAUTIONS, OR SECURITIES, DEMANDED FROM THEM.

Inst. Lib. IV. Tit. 10, 11.
Hoppii *Comm.* Lib. IV. Tit. 10, 11.
Heinecc. *A. R.* ⎫ Lib. IV. Tit.
——— *El. J. C.* ⎭ 10, 11.
Wood's *Inst. of the Civ. Law.* B. IV. ch. 1. 3.
Wood's *Inst. of the Laws of England.* B. IV. ch. 1. 4.
Blackstone's *Comm.* B. III. ch. 3, 18, 19.

1. BY the ancient Roman Law, no action or exception could be brought in the name of *another*; but every suitor was obliged to prosecute or defend his suit *in person*. The same practice obtained by the common law of England, unless dispensed with by special licence from the Crown[1].

2. A way was afterwards introduced of using the help of others, in prosecuting or defending a suit; by feigning that the dominion or property of the suit was transferred on them; and by ordering that all acts in the progress of the cause should be directed to and against them, instead of the

[1] The same practice also formerly obtained, and, unless dispensed with, still obtains, in the Courts of the University of Cambridge. See Appendix, No. v. vi.

principals. The persons so employed were called *procuratores*, or *proctors*.

3. A proctor is one, who administers the affairs of another, at the mandate, or commission, of the principal.

4. A proctor was, 1. Extrajudicial, otherwise called a mandatee[1]. 2. Judicial, appointed to manage a civil suit or action at law. He who, without commission, undertook the defence of a *reus*, that was absent, was called *defensor*.

5. To the judicial proctor of the Romans answers an attorney at law in England; who is empowered, by several statutes, to act in the place or *turn* of another, and to manage his matters of law.

6. In order that judgments might not be eluded, certain cautions, or securities, were given by the litigant parties, or their respective proctors; which were called, 1. *Judicatum solvi*. 2. *De judicio sisti*. 3. *De rato*. By the first the suitor engaged, if he lost his cause, to pay whatever sum he should be condemned in, by the judge: by the second, he gave security to continue in court, and abide the sentence: the third was peculiar to a proctor or defensor; by which it was engaged, that the principal should confirm whatever such proctor or defensor should do in his name.

7. Cautions, with respect to the manner in which they were taken, were of four kinds. 1. *Cautio fidejussoria*. 2. *Pignoratitia*. 3. *Juratoria*. 4. *Nude promissoria*. Of these the first was generally in use, and called by way of eminence, *Satisdatio*.

[1] See Book II. ch. 18. pr. 16—19.

8. By the old law, neither the actor nor his proctor, when there was no doubt concerning his mandate, gave caution at all. In real actions, the *reus* gave the caution *judicatum solvi;* and the same security was required from his proctor: but in personal actions, the *reus*, who defended the suit in his own name, was excused. A defensor of the *reus* not only gave the caution *judicatum solvi*, but that *de rato* besides.

9. By the new law, an actor gave caution to contest the suit, within two months after porrecting his libel; and, if he lost his cause, to pay a tenth of the sum, charged in that libel, by way of costs. A *reus*, whether convened in a real or personal action, gave the caution *judicio sisti*.

10. The proctor of an actor, when his mandate was doubtful, gave the caution *de rato*. The proctor of a *reus*, when the *reus* himself was present, gave no caution: when the *reus* was absent, he gave the caution *judicatum solvi*.

11. The practice of the Courts of Common Law in England, in *formerly* demanding from the plaintiff *nominal pledges of prosecution*, and in *still* demanding from the defendant what is called *special bail*, is not unlike the *satisdations*, required from an actor and reus by the Roman Laws.

CHAPTER IV.

OF ACTIONS PERPETUAL AND TEMPORARY.

Inst. Lib. IV. Tit. 12.
Hoppii *Comm.* Lib. IV. Tit. 12.
Heinecc. *A. R.* } Lib. IV. Tit. 12.
——— *El. J. C.* } Lib. IV. Tit. 12.
Wood's *Inst. of the Civ. Law.* B. III. ch. 11.
Wood's *Inst. of the Laws of England.* B. IV. ch. 4.
Blackstone's *Comm.* B. III. ch. 20.

1. No certain time was assigned by the ancient Roman Law, within which actions might be brought; but all were *perpetual,* in the proper sense of that word. Afterward, those actions only were called perpetual, which did not expire till after *thirty* years; and others, limited to a shorter time, were denominated *temporary.*

2. Real actions, whether civil or prætorian, continued as long as the *jus in re,* from whence such actions arose; or else were perpetual, and lasted thirty years. Personal actions, civil and prætorian, whether arising from contracts or offences; as also the actions denominated mixt; were, generally, perpetual.

3. Penal actions, when civil, were perpetual; when prætorian, were annual: but with some exceptions, in both cases.

4. In criminal prosecutions, the right of accusing was, ordinarily, limited to twenty years.

5. By the Common Law of England, all actions are perpetual; no certain time being assigned, beyond which they may not be brought. But a precise time hath been fixed by several Acts of Parliament, called the *Statutes of Limitation;* which may be pleaded by the defendant *in bar* of the plaintiff's demand.

6. Actions, like other rights, descended, in many cases, to a man's heirs. This might be, 1. Actively, when granted *to* the heirs of the actor. 2. Passively, when allowed *against* the heirs of the *reus.*

7. Real actions, and such as were persecutory of the thing, whether arising from contracts or offences, were granted, actively and passively, *to* heirs and *against* them. Penal actions were granted *to* heirs, but not *against* them; unless suit had been contested during the life of the *reus.*

8. If the actor, before sentence past, could any way be satisfied, the *reus* was absolved.

9. By the law of England, the death of either of the litigant parties is an abatement of the suit. Personal actions, arising *ex contractu,* may be revived by and against executors: those arising *ex delicto* die with the person.

CHAPTER V.

OF EXCEPTIONS AND REPLICATIONS.

Inst. Lib. IV. Tit. 13, 14.	Wood's *Inst. of the Civ. Law.* B. IV. ch. 3.
Hoppii *Comm.* Lib. IV. Tit. 13, 14.	Wood's *Inst. of the Laws of England.* B. IV. ch. 4.
Heinecc. *A. R.* / ——— *El. J. C.* } Lib. IV. Tit. 13, 14.	Blackstone's *Comm.* B. III. ch. 20.

1. An action, brought by the actor, might be stopt or stayed, by opposing to it, on the part of the *reus*, what was called an exception.

2. An exception might be opposed two ways. 1. By *denying* the cause of complaint; either simply, or with the allegation of new matter: by which the action was excluded *ipso jure*. 2. By *confessing* the action to be just, according to strict right, but eluding the force of it, from a principle of equity. The former sort were called exceptions to the fact; the latter, exceptions to the action.

3. Exceptions, with regard to their origin, were 1. Civil. 2. Prætorian. With regard to their effects, they were, 1. Perpetual. 2. Temporary.

4. Perpetual (otherwise denominated peremptory) exceptions were those, which totally repelled and extinguished the actions, to which they were opposed.

5. Perpetual exceptions were sometimes so called, with respect to time: in which sense all exceptions were, regularly, perpetual; though the actions, to which they were opposed, were temporary.

6. Temporary (otherwise denominated dilatory) exceptions were those, which delayed and barred an action for a time.

7. When the *reus* had made his exception, the actor might oppose it by what was called a replication. The answer of the *reus* to a replication was called a duplication. The answer of the actor to a duplication was called a triplication: and if the *reus* had any thing further to oppose to this, it was called a quadruplication.

8. In the laws of England, the several altercations between the plaintiff and defendant are denominated pleadings. Of these the first is the declaration, made by the plaintiff, setting forth his cause of complaint. To which are opposed, on the part of the defendant, 1. A defence, or denial of the complaint. 2. An excuse, or plea.

9. Pleas are, 1. Dilatory, which tend to delay or put off the suit. 2. Pleas to the action, which go to the merits of the complaint.

10. Dilatory pleas are, 1. To the jurisdiction. 2. To the disability of the plaintiff. 3. In abatement.

11. Pleas to the action are, 1. General, denying at once the whole declaration; and called the general issue. 2. Special, advancing some new fact, not mentioned in the declaration, in bar of the plaintiff's demand.

12. When the defendant has made his plea, the plaintiff may oppose it by what is called a replication. The answer of the defendant to a replication is called a rejoinder. The answer of the plaintiff to a rejoinder is called a sur-rejoinder. The answer, made by the defendant, to a sur-rejoinder, is called a rebutter: and if the plaintiff has any thing further to oppose to this, it is called a sur-rebutter.

CHAPTER VI.

OF INTERDICTS.

Inst. Lib. IV. Tit. 15.
Hoppii *Comm.* Lib. IV. Tit. 15.
Heinecc. *A. R.* / —— *El. J. C.* } Lib. IV. Tit. 15.
Wood's *Inst. of the Civ. Law.* B. IV. ch. 3.
Wood's *Inst. of the Laws of England.* B. IV. ch. 4.
Blackstone's *Comm.* B. IV. ch. 10. 27.

1. INTERDICTS were so called, because interposed, in the nature of an interlocutory decree, between two parties contending for possession, till the property could be tried.

2. Interdicts, by the old Roman Law, were precepts, issued by the prætor, in a certain form of words; by which he ordered or forbad something to be done, in a cause concerning possession or *quasi*-possession.

3. Interdicts, by the later law, were extraordinary actions, by which the possession or *quasi*-possession of a thing in dispute was summarily decided.

4. Possession was, 1. Natural. 2. Civil.

5. Interdicts were, 1. Prohibitory; which prohibited something from being done. 2. Restoratory; which commanded something to be restored. 3. Exhibitory; which commanded some thing or person to be exhibited.

6. Interdicts were granted, in order that possession might be, 1. Gained. 2. Retained. 3. Recovered.

7. Interdicts for the purpose of *gaining* possession were, 1. *Quorum bonorum;* when goods belonging to an inheritance were unlawfully withheld from the *bonorum possessor.* 2. *Quod legatorum;* when a legacy had been seized by the legatee, without consent of the heir. 3. *Salvianum;* when goods had been obligated by the hirer of a rural estate, as a security to the letter for payment of rent.

8. Interdicts for the purpose of *retaining* possession were, 1. *Uti possidetis;* granted to him, who at the time of contesting suit was in possession of an immoveable, in order that he might be declared the legal possessor. 2. *Utrubi;* granted for the like purpose to him, who at the time of contesting suit was in possession of a moveable.

9. The interdict for the purpose of *recovering* possession was called *unde vi;* granted to him, who had been ejected from the possession of an immoveable by force.

10. Interdicts were, 1. Single; in which each of the litigant parties sustained one character, either of actor or *reus.* 2. Double; in which each of the litigant parties sustained two characters, both of actor and *reus.*

11. Injunctions in England, issued from the Courts of Chancery and Exchequer, to stop proceedings at law, to stay waste, or to quiet possession of lands; and the actions called possessory; partake of the nature of interdicts according to the Roman Law.

CHAPTER VII.

OF THE METHODS, BY WHICH THE TEMERITY OF LITIGANTS WAS RESTRAINED.

Inst. Lib. IV. Tit. 16.
Hoppii *Comm.* Lib. IV. Tit. 16.
Heinecc. *A. R.* } Lib. IV. Tit. 16.
——— *El. J. C.* }

Wood's *Inst. of the Civ. Law.* B. IV. ch. 1.
Burn's *Eccl. Law.* Titles, *Advocate. Oaths.*

1. THE temerity of litigants was restrained, 1. By the oath of calumny. 2. By a pecuniary mulct. 3. By the fear of legal infamy.

2. The oath of calumny was, 1. General: taken, at the beginning of the suit, by the actor, *reus*, and their respective advocates; who severally swore, they believed their cause to be just. 2. Special; otherwise called the oath of malice: demandable at any time during the suit, on suspicion of malice in the party from whom required.

3. The oath of calumny was formerly taken in England, in causes civil and ecclesiastical; and may yet be required in the courts, which are governed by the Civil and Canon Laws[1].

4. An actor, if unable to make good his charge, was punished by a pecuniary mulct; which, before

[1] It is actually required in the University Courts at Cambridge. See Appendix, No. IV.

the age of Justinian, was a tenth of the sum, demanded in his libel. But, by a constitution of that emperor, the party, who either prosecuted or defended a cause without just grounds, was condemned to pay the costs of suit.

5. Infamy is the loss of reputation: and arose, 1. From fact; in the opinion of good men. 2. From law; *ipso jure*, or by the sentence of the judge.

6. Legal infamy was incurred, whenever a person was condemned on account of some offence or fraud; or in an action arising from any of the four contracts called ***Depositum*, *Societas*, *Mandatum*, *Tutela*.**

CHAPTER VIII.

OF THE OFFICE OF A JUDGE.

Inst. Lib. IV. Tit. 17.
Hoppii *Comm.* Lib. IV. Tit. 17.
Heinecc. *A. R.* Lib. IV. Tit. 6, pr. § 1—6. 9, 10. 39—41. Tit. 17, pr. § 1—4.
——— *El. J. C.* Lib. IV. Tit. 17.
Wood's *Inst. of the Civ. Law.* B. IV. ch. 1. 3.
Esprit des Loix. Liv. VI. ch. 3, 4. Liv. XI. ch. 18.
Noodt de Jurisdictione.
Cowell, *Inst. Juris Anglicani.* Lib. IV. Tit. 17.
Wood's *Inst. of the Laws of England.* B. IV. ch. 3, 4.
Blackstone's *Comm.* B. IV. ch. 7 B. II. ch. 12. 20. B. III. ch. 1. 4. 21. 23.

1. A JUDGE is a person appointed by authority to hear and determine causes, civil and criminal.

2. The power of judging civil causes, among the Romans, belonged at first to the kings; and, after their expulsion, to the consuls: the persons, on whom it next devolved, were the prætor, at Rome, and the proconsuls and *præsides*, in the provinces.

I.

3. During the Roman Republic, the offices of magistrate and judge were distinct and separate. A magistrate was appointed *cum jurisdictione et imperio;* to a judge belonged only *nuda notio, sine jurisdictione et imperio.*

4. Jurisdiction is the power of hearing and determining causes, and of doing justice in matters of complaint. It is divided into, 1. Voluntary and contentious. 2. Civil and criminal. 3. Ordinary and extraordinary. 4. Proper and delegated.

5. *Imperium* is, 1. *Merum*, the simple power of punishment. 2. *Mixtum*, the power of punishment, with some degree of jurisdiction.

6. *Notio* is the power of hearing causes, and of pronouncing sentence, without any degree of jurisdiction.

7. The office of the magistrate was to enquire into matters of law; and whatever business was transacted before him, was said to be done *in jure*. The office of the judge was to enquire into matters of fact; and whatever was transacted before him, was said to be done *in judicio*. When the magistrate took cognizance both of the law and the fact, he was said to administer justice *extra ordinem;* and the judgment, so administered, was called extraordinary.

8. The magistrate, when he decided on matters of law, was assisted by a council of ten, called *Decemviri litibus judicandis*. To these was added, in important cases, another council of 105 persons, selected from each tribe; whose judgment was final, and called *Judicium centumvirale*.

9. In England, different tribunals are appointed for determining issues of law and of fact. An issue on matter of law is called a demurrer, and is tried by the judges of the court, before whom the action is brought: an issue on matter of fact is determined by other methods, of which the principal is the trial by jury.

10. When the litigant parties had agreed on a proper person to examine the fact, the prætor was applied to, by the actor, to appoint him: and the person, so appointed, was called *judex datus sive pedaneus.*

11. A judge had properly the cognizance of actions, that were *stricti juris:* in actions *bonæ fidei*, or of the arbitrary kind, the person appointed was called *arbiter*. When the action was laid for the recovery of some certain thing, demanded by the actor, the persons, given by the prætor, were called *recuperatores.*

12. The judge, given by the prætor, might be rejected by either of the litigants, who disapproved the appointment: in like manner as jurors in England may be *challenged*, by either party, as they appear, when called, to be sworn.

13. The cause being fully heard, the judge pronounced sentence; the execution of which was committed to officers, appointed for the purpose.

14. In causes *bonæ fidei*, and such as were arbitrary, the parties sometimes agreed to submit the matter in dispute to a third person; in which case, a deposit of money was generally made, to be forfeited by him, who refused to stand by such person's sentence. This mode of ending a suit is called, in the Roman Law, *compromissum*, and, in the law of England, arbitration; and the decision of the arbitrators, or of the umpire, is called an award. When the litigant parties agreed upon a satisfaction among themselves, without referring it to arbitration, it was called, in the Roman Law, transaction; and in the law of England, it is called an accord.

II.

15. After the decline of the Roman republic, the offices of magistrate and judge were united: by which means all judgments became extraordinary, and the distinction of what was done *in jure* and *in judicio* was abolished[1].

16. The office of a judge, regarded as a magistrate, was, 1. *Merum sive nobile.* 2. *Promotum sive mercenarium.*

17. To the exercise of the judicial office were required, 1. *Causæ cognitio;* or an enquiry into the truth and justice of the matter in controversy. 2. *Judicatio,* or the pronouncing of sentence.

18. In real actions, when sentence was given against the actor, or demandant, the *reus*, or person in possession, was discharged: when sentence was given against the *reus*, he was obliged to restore not only the thing itself, but all its fruits and produce.

19. In actions *ad exhibendum*, the *reus*, if condemned, was bound not only to exhibit the thing itself, but also to exhibit it in the same state it was, when first the exhibition was demanded.

20. In the actions called *Judicia Divisoria;* (viz. *Familiæ Erciscundæ, Communi Dividundo, Finium Regundorum*) each of the claimants was to have his respective part; or, if that could not be done, he, who had the advantage, was ordered to render an equivalent in money.

[1] In general it may be observed, that in the Institutions, the Code and the Novels, *judex* and *magistratus* denote the same person: and in the Pandects or Digests, whenever the word *judex* is mentioned alone, *judex pedaneus* is to be understood.

21. In England, the partition of an inheritance may be by consent of the coheirs; or by Bill in Equity. In determining the boundaries of contiguous lordships, the writ *de Perambulatione facienda*[2] is of the same use as the *Judicium Finium Regundorum* in the Roman Law, although it is seldom used.

22. A judge, in England, is a chief magistrate, appointed by the Crown, to try causes, civil and criminal, and to do what to justice appertains, according to the law and custom of the land.

[2] The writs *de Partitione facienda*, and *de Rationabilibus divisis*, are abolished by 3 and 4 William IV. c. 27.

CHAPTER IX.

OF THE FORM OF PRIVATE JUDGMENTS, OR THE COURSE OF PROCEEDING IN CIVIL CAUSES, ACCORDING TO THE ROMAN LAW.

Hoppii *Comm.* Lib. IV. Tit. 6. § 11. Heinecc. *A. R.* Lib. IV. Tit. 21. § 2, 3, 4. Lib. IV. Tit. 6. § 7, 8. 11—22. 42, 43. Tit. 17. § 5—13. Wood's *Inst. of the Civ. Law.* B. IV. ch. 1, 2, 3.

Wood's *Inst. of the Laws of Eng.* B. IV. ch. 4. Burn's *Eccl. Law.* Titles, *Notary Public, Oaths.* Blackstone's *Comm.* B. III. ch. 3. 18, 19, 20, 22, 23, 24, 25, 26.

1. JUDICIUM, or trial, is a legal debate, on a matter of controversy, before a competent judge.

2. Judgments, in the Roman Law, were, 1. Private. 2. Public.

3. Private judgments were those, which related to civil causes; in order to redress an injury, as it affected an individual; and were prosecuted by action, which could only be instituted by the injured party.

4. A court is a place where justice is judicially administered. This place, among the Romans, was, 1. Superior. 2. Plane. In the former, the prætor administered justice *pro tribunali:* in the latter, he was said *de plano cognoscere.*

5. To a court three persons at least are necessary, *actor, reus, judex.* To whom may be added 1. Advocates or counsel. 2. Proctors. 3. Notaries.

4. Apparitors or bedels; called *viatores* and *executores litium.*

6. The Roman prætor was not allowed to hear causes, but on certain days. Days were, 1. *Fasti.* 2. *Nefasti.* 3. *Intercisi.* Of these the first were properly judicial, and were called *dies sessionum, dies legitimi,* or term-days.

7. The constituent parts of a civil cause, according to the form of private judgments, were, in order these. I. *Vocatio in jus.* II. *Postulatio et editio actionis.* III. *Vadimonium.* IV. *Intentio litis sive actionis.* V. *Exceptio rei.* VI. *Datio judicis.* VII. *Satisdationes actoris et rei.* VIII. *Contestatio litis.* IX. Oaths of the judge and litigants. X. Proofs. XI. *Disceptatio causæ.* XII. Sentence. XIII. Execution. XIV. Appeal.

8, I. *Vocatio in jus* was a personal citation of the *reus,* or offending party, by which he was commanded to appear before the magistrate, or prætor, in order to enter into suit.

9. Personal citation, by the law of the Twelve Tables, might be by private authority, and with force; but could not be executed upon a man, within his own house or walls. The same protection against an arrest is afforded to a defendant, in England. If the *reus* absconded, so that the citation was of no effect, the actor was sent into the possession of his goods.

10. In England, the beginning or foundation of a civil[1] suit is by a writ, 1. Of summons, which may be followed by a writ of *distringas,* if the party

[1] See 2 William IV. c. 39. An act for uniformity of process in personal actions.

cannot be served personally. 2. Of *capias*, when the party is arrested and held to bail.

11. If the *reus* could find sureties, who offered to defend his person (which sureties were called *vindices*); or the parties could make up the matter by transaction, while they were *in the way* to the magistrate; the *reus* was dismissed. In England, a defendant, before he made his plea, might have demanded an imparlance[1] with the plaintiff, to see if the matter could not be ended without further suit.

12. II. *Postulatio actionis* was the actor's asking of leave to institute his action, on appearance of the parties before the prætor.

13. *Editio actionis* was the publishing of the action by the actor in the presence of the *reus*, after leave asked and obtained of the prætor.

14. III. *Vadimonium conceptum* was the actor's obliging of the *reus* to give sureties for his appearance before the prætor, on a day appointed. Such sureties were called *vades*.

15. The day appointed was generally the third day after the present, called *dies perendinus*: but sometimes a long interval was allowed by the prætor.

16. On default of either party on the day appointed, the defaulter lost his cause.

17. In England, a day is always given for the parties to appear in court, in person or by their attornies, from one adjournment to another: which giving of a day is called the *continuance*. In case of omission or neglect by the plaintiff, he loses the benefit of his writ, and is said to be *nonsuit*ed, or

[1] Imparlances are now abolished.

nonpros'd; when the omission or neglect is on the part of the defendant, judgment may go against him for such default.

18. IV. *Intentio litis sive actionis* was the preferring of the suit or action, in a certain form of words, by the actor; on his own appearance, and that of the *reus*, before the prætor.

19. To this succeeded, V. *Exceptio rei;* or the exception made to the action, by the *reus*. VI. *Datio judicis;* or the appointment of a judge, by the prætor, to try the fact; who at the same time defined the number of witnesses, by whom the fact should be proved. VII. *Satisdationes Actoris et Rei;* or the cautions and securities given by each of the litigants: all already explained[2].

20. VIII. *Contestatio litis* answers to what in the law of England is called joining issue; being a narration of the controversy, made by each party, before the judge, in the presence of witnesses: by which the matter in dispute was brought to a trial, and in a way of being determined, in favour of the actor or the *reus*.

21. Whatever preceded the contestation of suit, was transacted before the prætor, and said to be done *in jure:* whatever was subsequent to it, was transacted before the judge, and said to be done in *judicio*.

22. IX. The oath of the judge was, that he would decide on the merits of the cause, *ex animi sententia:* that, taken by the litigants, was the oath of calumny[3].

[2] See Chapters 3d, 5th, and 8th of this Book.

[3] See Chapter 7th of this Book.

23. If on the day appointed for trial the judge were hindered from attending, *dies diffindebatur*, or the day was deferred: if either of the litigants were absent, he was cited by one or more edicts; after which, if he did not appear, the cause was heard, and sentence given, as if he had been present.

24. X. Proofs are derived from facts; and were always first required from the side, which *affirmed* the matter in question.

25. Proof (*probatio*) was, 1. *Plena;* by two witnesses, or a public instrument. 2. *Semi-plena;* by one witness, or a private instrument. Two half proofs, joined together, made a full proof.

26. Proofs might be had from, (1) Confession; (2) Presumptions; (3) Witnesses; (4) Instruments; (5) Oaths.

27. (1) Confession is an acknowledgment by the adverse party, that the debt or allegation with which he is charged, is true.

28. (2) Presumptions are conjectural conclusions from probable arguments: and are, 1. Of law. 2. Of man.

29. (3) Witnesses are persons called upon to declare in court what they know of the fact under examination.

30. To make *full* proof, two witnesses were necessary: and where one only was to be had, the party himself was sometimes examined in his own behalf. In England, one witness is sufficient to testify to a single fact: nor can any one be witness in his own cause.

31. The examination of witnesses was formerly in public, and *viva voce:* but, according to the

modern practice of the Courts of Civil Law, it is now in private; interrogatories being previously settled for the purpose.

32. Unwilling witnesses might be *compelled* to declare their testimony: in England, they may be brought in by a writ of *subpœna ad testificandum.*

33. Trial by witnesses, without the intervention of a jury, is in one instance permitted by the law of England; on a writ of dower brought by a wife, when the death of the husband is in issue.

34. (4) Instruments or writings were, 1. Public; which proved themselves. 2. Private; which, unless very ancient, were to be proved by witnesses.

35. In England, records, and deeds of thirty years, prove themselves. Modern deeds, and other writings, must be proved by witnesses. But books of account are not allowed to be given in evidence for the owner; as in the Civil Law.

36. (5) Oaths are, 1. Promissory. 2. Decisive.

37. The decisive oath is, 1. Voluntary. 2. Judicial. 3. Necessary. The necesary oath is, 1. Purgatory; 2. Suppletory[1].

38. To the decisive judicial oath, in use among the Romans, that species of trial in England, which was called wager[2] of law, was somewhat similar: by

[1] See the case of *Williams* and Lady *Bridget Osborne*, in *Burn's* Ecclesiastical Law, Title, *Oaths. Williams* was admitted, by the Dean of the Arches, to his suppletory oath, in order to prove his marriage with Lady *Bridget:* upon which the Lady appealed to the delegates; by whom the marriage was confirmed.

[2] It is enacted by 3 and 4 William IV. c. 42. § 13, "that no wager of law shall hereafter be allowed."

which, in an action of debt upon simple contract, a defendant, who would swear himself not chargeable, and who appeared to be a person of credit, was acquitted of his debt.

39. XI. *Disceptatio causæ* was the disputing of the cause by the *patroni*, or advocates, on both sides. This consisted of two parts. 1. *Conjectio causæ*. 2. *Peroratio*.

40. XII. *Sentence* is, 1. Interlocutory, on some incident question, arising from the principal cause. 2. Definitive, (otherwise called final) by which the principal cause is determined.

41. Sentence, in the law of England, is called the judgment; which cannot be *entered* till the next term after trial had, and upon notice to the vanquished party.

42. To a sentence costs are a necessary appendage, both in the Roman and English Laws.

43. XIII. *Execution* is the putting in force the sentence of the judge.

44. By the old Roman Law, if the party, who was cast, did not obey the sentence within thirty days, he was assigned over to the actor; who might commit him to prison, till satisfaction was made: this was called *addictio*. But the general way was for the prætor to cause execution to be done by lictors; who obliged all to make the satisfaction required, in damages, or by giving pledges.

45. By the laws of England, execution, in action of ejectment, is effected by writ of *Habere facias possessionem*. In other actions, where the judgment is, that something special be done by the defendant, a special writ of execution is issued, according to

the case. Where money only is recovered, executions are, 1. Against the body of the defendant; or against his bail. 2. Against his goods. 3. Against his goods, and profits of his lands. 4. Against his goods, and possession of his lands. 5. Against his body, lands and goods.

46. XIV. *Appeal* is the removing of a cause from an inferior to the next superior court; an inhibition being issued to the inferior judge to stop proceedings, while the appeal is depending.

47. An appeal might be made immediately, *apud acta;* or within ten days after sentence passed, by libel. After two appeals in the same cause, a *third* was not allowed.

48. *Supplication* is a complaint, brought within two years against a sentence; where the person, against whom the sentence was pronounced, neglected to appeal in time.

49. *Restitutio in integrum* was, when a cause, on petition of the party who was cast, was reduced by the prætor to its first state; after which, the suit might come on again, and have a second hearing.

50. A *review* is a petition to the same judge to rehear the cause, and rectify the sentence, if there be occasion.

51. In England, after judgment given, execution may be staid by several writs[1], in the nature of appeals: of which the principal are, 1. A writ of *Audita querela.* 2. A writ of error.

[1] Writs of attaint are abolished by 6 George IV. c. 50.

CHAPTER X.

OF THE COURTS IN ENLGAND, IN WHICH THE CIVIL LAW IS PERMITTED TO BE USED.

Wood's *Inst. of the Laws of England.* B. IV. ch. 1, 2.
Grey's *Ecclesiastical Law*, Title 22. 24. 32. 42—46.
Oughtoni *Ordo Judiciorum.* Tit. 137. 157—192. 193—217. 218—258. 259—268.
Burn's *Eccl. Law.* Titles, *Advowson, Appeal, Archdeacon, Arches. Benefice. Chancellor, Colleges, Commissary, Consistory, Consultation, Courts. Defamation, Degradation, Delegates, Deprivation, Dilapidations, Double Quarrel. Excommunication. Faculty Court. Marriage. Peculiar, Penance, Prerogative Court, Prohibition. Sequestration, Spoliation, Suspension. Tithes. Visitation. Wills.*
Blackstone's *Comm.* Introduction. Sect. 1. 3. B. I. ch. 2. 18. B. II. ch. 3. art. 2. ch. 20. B. III. ch. 3. 5, 6, 7. 16. 22. art. 3. B. IV. ch. 19.
Browne, A. LL.D. *Compendious View of the Law of the Admiralty.*

1. THERE are four courts in England, in which the Civil Law is permitted, under different restrictions, to be used. These are, I. The Court Military, or Court of Honour. II. The Courts Maritime. III. Courts Christian, or Ecclesiastical Courts. IV. The Courts of the two Universities.

2. I. The Court Military, or Court of Honour, in great vogue in the ages of chivalry, is now almost out of use. The judges of this court were the Lord High Constable and Earl Marshal, jointly; but it

is now held before the Earl Marshal only: it is not a court of record.

3. Causes, cognizable in the Military Court, relate, 1. To matters of honour. 2. To matters of heraldry and coat-armour. But no cause is cognizable here, that may be determined by the Common Law; nor can any pecuniary satisfaction be given to the party injured, in the way of damages.

4. The proceedings in this court are conformed to the Civil Law, and the Law of Arms: and from its sentence an appeal lies to the King in person.

5. II. The Courts Maritime are, 1. The Court of Admiralty; which is twofold, (1) The Instance Court; (2) The Prize Court; and is held before the Lord High Admiral, or his deputy, who is called the judge. It is not a court of record. 2. Its Courts of Appeal.

6. Causes, cognizable in the Courts Maritime, are those arising on the sea; but not partly on the sea, and partly on the land; nor within the body of any county.

7. The proceedings in this court are much conformed to the Civil Law, in conjunction with marine customs: but in criminal cases, offences are tried by commissioners, the judge of the admiralty presiding; and the law of England is followed, as if the offences had been committed on land.

8. The Courts of Appeal, belonging to the Courts of Admiralty, are, 1. The King in Council[1]. 2. In causes of prize[2] taken at sea, certain commissioners of appeal.

[1] See 2 and 3 William IV. c. 92; and 3 and 4 William IV. c. 41.

[2] See 3 and 4 William IV. c. 41. § 2 and 31.

9. III. The separation of the ecclesiastical from the temporal courts was no where known, till after the emperors became Christian; nor in England, till after the Norman conquest.

10. Ecclesiastical Courts are, 1. Courts of Voluntary. 2. Courts of Contentious Jurisdiction.

11. Of Courts of Voluntary Jurisdiction, the chief is the Faculty Court, belonging to the Archbishop of Canterbury: the judge of which is called Master or Commissary of the Faculties.

12. Courts of Contentious Jurisdiction are, 1. The Court of the Archdeacon: the judge of which, where he does not preside himself, is called the official. 2. The Consistory Court of every bishop in his diocese: the judge of which is, (1) The bishop's chancellor; or, (2) His commissary. 3. The Court of Arches, belonging to the archbishop: the judge of which is called the Dean of the Arches. 4. The Court of Peculiars; having jurisdiction over all such parishes in the Province of Canterbury, which are subject to the metropolitan only. 5. The Prerogative Court, for the trial of testamentary causes, where the party dying hath left *bona notabilia* in two different dioceses: the judge of which is called the Judge of the Prerogative. 6. The great Court of Appeal[1] in all ecclesiastical causes. The sentence of this court is definitive.

13. The Courts of Ecclesiastical Jurisdiction are, none of them, Courts of Record.

14. Causes, cognizable in Ecclesiastical Courts,

[1] See 2 and 3 William IV. c. 92; and 3 and 4 William IV. c. 41.

are, 1. Beneficial. 2. Matrimonial. 3. Testamentary. 4. Criminal[2].

15. Beneficial causes are, 1. *Duplex querela.* 2. *Jus patronatus.* 3. Spoliation. 4. Dilapidations. 5. Non-payment of ecclesiastical dues. 6. Subtraction of tithes. Tithes are, 1. Predial. 2. Personal. 3. Mixt: which are due of common right to the parson or vicar; unless discharged, (1) By real composition, (2) By prescription.

16. Matrimonial causes are, 1. Jactitation of marriage. 2. Contract of marriage. 3. Restitution of conjugal rights. 4. Divorces: (1) *a vinculo matrimonii*, for a canonical cause existing *previous* to the marriage. (2) *A mensa et thoro*, for a cause arising after marriage; as adultery, cruelty, &c. 5. Alimony.

17. Testamentary causes are, 1. Probate of wills. 2. Granting of administrations. 3. Subtraction of legacies[3].

18. Criminal causes are those, which relate to crimes of ecclesiastical cognizance: where the proceedings arc *pro saluto animæ et reformatione morum.*

19. The punishment of crimes of ecclesiastical cognizance belongs, of common right, to the bishops, and their vicars general in spirituals; and, by concessions or prescription, to archdeacons also: to both whom is committed, for this purpose, the power of visitation.

20. Ecclesiastical punishments are, 1. Common to clergy and laity. 2. Peculiar to the clergy.

[2] Under criminal causes I include those called defamatory; which Oughton, in his *Ordo Judiciorum*, reckons as a fifth species of ecclesiastical causes, distinct from criminal.

[3] See 3 Haggard's *Eccl. Rep.* p. 161.

21. Ecclesiastical punishments, common to clergy and laity, are 1. Monition. 2. Penance. 3. Excommunication. Those peculiar to the clergy, are, 1. Sequestration of the profits of a church. 2. Suspension. 3. Deprivation. 4. Degradation.

22. Appeals in causes ecclesiastical, which formerly, from the reign of Stephen to that of Henry VIII., lay to the Pope or See of Rome, are now (by 24 Henry VIII. c. 12, 25 Henry VIII. c. 19, and 2 and 3 William IV. c. 92,) directed to be in this form, and not otherwise: from the archdeacon or his official, to the bishop or diocesan: from the bishop, his chancellor or commissary, to the archbishop of the province: from the Court of Arches, Court of Peculiars, and the Prerogative Court, to the King in Council.

23. IV. The Universities of Oxford and Cambridge are corporations, lay and civil, by prescription; whose charters and privileges have been confirmed by parliament.

24. Of the privileges belonging to the Universities the chief are, 1. The reservation of a certain part of the rent, arising from college leases, in provision-corn. 2. The printing of bibles and books of common prayer; and (in the University of Cambridge) of acts of parliament, and abridgments of acts of parliament[1]; in concurrence with the King's printers.

[1] This valuable privilege, of printing acts of parliament and abridgments of acts of parliament, was solemnly confirmed to the University of Cambridge, by the unanimous judgment of the Court of King's Bench, Nov. 24, 1758. See *Burn's* Ecclesiastical Law, Title, *Colleges:* where the whole learning on this subject is exhausted, in an incomparable argument, in behalf of the University, by the late Lord Chancellor Yorke, then Solicitor General.

3. The sending of two of their own body burgesses to parliament. 4. Presentation to benefices of Roman catholic patrons. 5. The Courts of the Chancellor of each University, or Vice-Chancellor; (which are also Courts of Record) in exclusion of the King's Courts of Common Law.

25. Causes, cognizable in the Chancellor's Courts of the two Universities, are all civil causes, excepting where the right of freehold is concerned; and all criminal offences and misdemesnors, under the degree of treason, felony, and mayhem.

26. To constitute the exclusive right of jurisdiction belonging to the Universities, one of the parties must be a scholar or privileged person: in which case, the Chancellor or Vice-Chancellor may claim cognizance of the cause, by certificate, without the intervention of a jury.

27. Besides the Chancellor's Courts, there is, in the University of Cambridge at least, another, called the Court of the Commissary: which hath cognizance in all causes, civil and criminal, within the University; unless where a Master of Arts, or one of superior degree, is a party.

28. The Courts of the Universities have power to punish for contempt and contumacy; to set a fine, and to imprison the party till it be paid; and to inflict ecclesiastical censures, or such as are appointed by the statutes, for offences that are merely temporal.

29. The trial of treason, felony, and mayhem, though prohibited in the Chancellor's Courts, is by a particular charter committed to the Courts of the High Steward of either University: to whom, and

to his deputy, is also given the privilege of holding a Court Leet.

30. From the sentence of the Chancellor or Vice-Chancellor, in the University of Oxford, an appeal lies to delegates, appointed by the congregation: from thence to other delegates, appointed by the Convocation: and if all three concur in the same sentence, it is final[1]. In case of discordance in the sentences, the appeal lies, in the last resort, to the King in Chancery, or to judges' delegates, appointed under the great seal.

31. From the sentence of the Chancellor or Vice-Chancellor, in the University of Cambridge, an appeal lies to the Senate, or body of the University; by whom the examination of the cause is committed to delegates, not less than three or more than five; whose sentence is final, and not liable to be reversed by *writ of error* from the Courts of Common Law. From the sentence of the Commissary an appeal lies to the Chancellor or Vice-Chancellor; and from thence to delegates, if the cause require it.

32. The right of appeal, allowed by the statutes of the Universities, extends to *all* causes[2], criminal as well as civil; in conformity to the Roman Law[3].

[1] This is agreeable to the Civil Law; according to which no appeal was admitted after *three* sentences conformable to each other. C. 7. 70. 1.

[2] See Appendix, No. II. III. for the Statutes of the University of Cambridge on this head.

[3] See D. 49. 1. 6. where the right of appeal in *criminal* causes is admitted in the Roman Law, without restriction, from the common principle of humanity. *Credo,* says Ulpian, *Humanitatis ratione, Omnem provocantem audiri debere.* And this, even though the person condemned wished to decline the benefit of

33. The four courts now mentioned, in which the Civil Law is permitted to be used, are all subordinate to the Courts of Common Law; and in case of encroachment of jurisdiction, are liable to be restrained by prohibition.

34. Prohibition is a writ, issuing out of some of the Courts of Common Law, forbidding the judge and parties of a suit in an inferior court to proceed in the prosecution; *on suggestion* that the cause originally, or on account of some collateral matter, does not belong to that jurisdiction.

35. When the matter suggested appears, in the judgment of the superior court, to be false, or not proved, a writ of consultation is granted; by which the cause is returned to the original jurisdiction, and determined by the court below.

the appeal, when made by another in his behalf. *Quid ergo si resistat, qui damnatus est, adversus provocationem; nec velit admittere ejus appellationem, perire festinans?* Adhuc putem differendum supplicium.

CHAPTER XI.

OF THE COURSE OF PROCEEDING IN THE ECCLESIASTICAL COURTS, AND COURTS OF THE TWO UNIVERSITIES, IN ENGLAND.

Grey's *Ecclesiastical Law*, Title 44, 45.

Oughtoni *Ordo Judiciorum*. Tit. 7. 14. 19. 24. 48. 54—61. 72, 73. 75. 80. 85. 95. 97. 104, 105. 110, 111. 113—123. 127. 131. 137—139. 150—156. 269—272. 274. 276, 277. 285. 288—293. 295. 303, 304. 307. 319, 320. 329. 330. *Synopsis Praxeos in Curiis Ecclesiasticis*, et *Ordo Judiciarius*; ad finem Tit. 14.

Burn's *Eccl. Law*. Titles, *Answer, Appeal. Citation. Evidence. Libel. Oaths.*

Blackstone's *Comm.* B. III. ch. 7.

Browne, A. LL.D. *Compendious View of the Civil Law.* Vol. I. *Practice of the Ecclesiastical Courts.*

Law, J. T. *Forms of Ecclesiastical Law.* 1831.

1. CAUSES, which may be moved in the Ecclesiastical Courts, in England, are, 1. Causes of office; which run in the name of the judge. 2. Of instance; at the solicitation of some party.

2. Causes of office are, 1. *Ex officio mero*. 2. *Ex officio promoto*. Causes of instance are, 1. Plenary. 2. Summary.

3. The constituent parts of an ecclesiastical cause, according to the usual course of proceedings, are, in order, these. I. Citation. II. Libel. III. Contestation of suit. IV. Personal answer of the defendant. V. Assignment of a term probatory. VI. Proofs. VII. Defensive allegation. VIII. Term to propound

all things. IX. Term to conclude. X. Informations. XI. Sentence. XII. Execution. XIII. Appeal.

4. I. Citation is a judicial act, by which the defendant is summoned to appear, in a place where justice is administered, in order to enter into suit.

5. Every citation or decree is returnable at a certain place and day. Such return is made, by certificate of the apparitor or other party serving the citation, verified by his affidavit. A decree is a citation, but more formal in its character. A decree *with intimation* instructs the party cited with the course to be adopted in default of appearance.

6. Besides the original or primary citation, there are others; called, 1. *Decretum viis et modis.* 2. *Sub mutuæ vicissitudinis obtentu,* or by letters of request.

7. II. A Libel (called in Common Law a *declaration,* and in Chancery a *bill*) is a charge, in writing, brought by the plaintiff; to which the defendant is obliged to answer.

8. The proceeding by libel is peculiar to causes of instance: in causes of office, the proceeding is by articles.

9. III. Contestation of suit is a general answer, made by the defendant; in which he denies the matter charged against him in the libel.

10. IV. Personal answer of the defendant is what is urged in particular, by way of denial or extenuation of the charge; *before* the plaintiff makes proof of his libel by witnesses.

11. The ecclesiastical judge might formerly have *compelled* the parties to answer *upon oath* to any matter objected against them, however criminal: but

the power of administering such oath (called the oath *ex officio*) is taken away, by the statute of 13 Car. II. Nor is any person now obliged to *purge* himself, upon oath, of any crime, of which he is accused.

12. V. The assignment of a term probatory is an appointment by the judge of a certain time, within which the plaintiff is required to *prove* so much of the libel, as the defendant has not confessed in his personal answers.

13. VI. Proofs are had, 1. From witnesses. 2. From instruments.

14. Witnesses are examined in private, 1. To the libel of the plaintiff. 2. To interrogatories, proposed by the defendant.

15. Unwilling witnesses may be brought in by a citation, called a *compulsory:* but those, who live at a distance, may be examined where they live, by virtue of a *commission.*

16. Instruments are, 1. Public. 2. Private. Which, if not confessed by the adverse party, must always be proved by the person who produces them.

17. When the term probatory lapses, before the plaintiff has finished his proof, it may be continued for a longer time, with the permission of the judge.

18. The plaintiff, having examined his witnesses in proof of his libel, demands publication of the depositions; this application is not granted, if the defendant asserts an allegation.

19. VII. Defensive allegation is what is opposed by the defendant, in writing, to the charge objected in the libel. To which are consequent, as in the case of the plaintiff, 1. The personal answer of the plaintiff. 2. A term probatory. 3. This ap-

plication is not granted if a responsive allegation is asserted.

20. VIII. The *term to propound all things* is an appointment by the judge of a time, at which both parties are to exhibit all the acts and instruments, which make for their respective causes.

21. IX. The *term to conclude* is an appointment by the judge of a time, at which both parties are understood to renounce all further exhibits and allegations, unless exceptive to the testimony of the witnesses.

22. The terms *to propound all things*, and *to conclude*, are peculiar to such causes as are plenary: in summary causes, instead of them, the term required is called the term *to hear sentence on the first assignation.*

23. X. Informations are arguments urged before the judge by the advocates on both sides, after the pleadings and proofs are concluded: which are followed by, XI. The sentence; either interlocutory or definitive: and, XII. Execution.

24. XIII. Sometimes a cause is removed from an inferior to a superior court; by which all proceedings in the lower court are suspended, till the reasons of such removal are heard.

25. A cause may be removed from an inferior to a superior court, 1. *Ante litis ingressum*, by provocation. 2. *Post litis ingressum*, by recusation. 3. By appeal.

26. Provocation is, when one, who suspects an inferior judge intends to proceed against him, in a cause of office or of instance, puts himself, *before* he is cited, under the protection of a superior court.

27. Recusation is, when one, who suspects an inferior judge of partiality, refuses, *after* he is cited, to submit to his jurisdiction: in which case, the person refusing must exhibit articles, to be referred to arbitrators, named on both sides.

28. Appeal is, 1. Judicial, or *apud acta;* which is made *viva voce.* 2. Extrajudicial, before a notary; which is made *in scriptis.*

29. Appeals may be, 1. From grievances, before sentence. 2. From the sentence.

30. [1]Appeals from grievances are *in scriptis;* and must be interposed within a certain time from the grievances committed.

31. [1]Appeals from the sentence are *apud acta,* or *viva voce,* at the time when sentence is pronounced; or *in scriptis,* within a certain time from the sentence.

32. In an appeal from the sentence, letters missive are demanded from the judge *a quo;* which are transmitted to the judge *ad quem,* to instruct him in the nature of the suit. Such letters missive are called, in the Civil Law, *Apostoli.*

33. In an appeal, whether from a *gravamen* or the sentence, an inhibition is issued from the superior court to the inferior, to stop proceedings.

34. If after inhibition issued, or appeal from the sentence, the judge *a quo,* or party obtaining sentence, shall *attempt* any act, in prejudice to the appellant, or the appeal; they may both be proceeded against *in causa Attentationis.*

[1] See 24 Henry VIII. c. 12. § 6, 7.

35. Appeals regularly were required to be finished within one year, called *primum fatale:* but sometimes a second year, called *secundum fatale*, was allowed.

36. The time of one or two years, allowed by law for the determination of appeals, is called *terminus juris:* in case a shorter time is appointed by the judge, that time is called *terminus hominis.*

37. In criminal causes of ecclesiastical cognizance, the methods of proceeding are, 1. By inquisition; *ex officio mero.* 2. By denunciation; or presentment of churchwardens. 3. By accusation; *ex officio promoto.*

38. The course of proceeding in the Courts of the two Universities is by citation, libel, &c. And the trial is, not by jury, but by examination of witnesses, informations, &c.[1] as in the Ecclesiastical and other Courts of the Civil Law.

[1] See Appendix, No. IV. V. VI.

CHAPTER XII.

OF PUBLIC JUDGMENTS.

Inst. Lib. IV. Tit. 18.
Hoppii *Comm.* Lib. IV. Tit. 18.
Heinecc. *A. R.* Lib. IV. Tit. 18. pr. § 1—10. 45—80.
——— *El. J. C.* Lib. IV. Tit. 18.
Wood's *Inst. of the Civ. Law.* B. III. ch. 10. B. IV. ch. 4.
Esprit des Loix. Liv. VI. ch. 11. 14. 15. 17—20. Liv. VII. ch. 10. 11. 13. Liv. XII. ch. 5—20.
Wood's *Inst. of the Laws of England.* B. III. ch. 1. 3. B. IV. ch. 5. art. 11. 12.
Blackstone's *Comm.* B. IV. ch. 15. B. II. ch. 3. B. III. ch. 8. B. IV. ch. 1. 4. 6. 9. 10. 11. 12. 14. 15. 17. 29.
Principles of Penal Law. Ch. 3—9. 12. 14. 15. 18—21.
Nuptiæ Sacræ.
De Lolme's *Constitution of England.*
Millar's *English Government.* Vol. I. and II.
Cottu, *On the Administration of Justice in England.*

1. PUBLIC offences, otherwise called crimes or misdemesnors, were punishable, among the Romans, by the laws concerning public judgments.

2. Public judgments were those, which related to crimes, declared to be public by some law; and might, regularly, be prosecuted by any one of the Roman people, though not particularly interested in the prosecution.

3. Public judgments answer to what in England is called Crown Law, where the prosecution is in the name of the king; the suits, so prosecuted, being called *Pleas of the Crown*.

4. Public judgments were distinguished from private, 1. In their institution. 2. In their exercise.

5. Besides public judgments, there were others, which were, 1. Extraordinary. 2. Popular.

6. Extraordinary judgments were those relating to crimes, concerning which no law was enacted, or no certain penalty was prescribed. The crimes, so circumstanced, were called extraordinary.

7. Popular judgments were those in which the mulct or penalty inflicted was applied to the private uses of any actor that would sue for it.

8. Of public judgments, some were, 1. Capital; in which the punishment prescribed was death; which death was, (1) Natural; such as took away the life of the criminal: (2) Civil; such as took away his liberty, or his citizenship. 2. Not capital; in which the punishment prescribed was short of death, natural or civil.

9. Punishments of natural or civil death were called capital: others, short of natural or civil death, were called not capital.

10. The modes of inflicting natural death were, 1. Hanging. 2. Precipitation from a rock. 3. Beheading. 4. Strangulation. 5. Burning alive. 6. Crucifixion, called *servile supplicium.* 7. *Damnatio ad furcam.* 8. *In gladium.* 9. *In bestias.* The dead body of the criminal was sometimes dissected, or hung in chains: but, generally, was buried, after leave obtained from the prince.

11. Civil death was, 1. Slavery. 2. *Damnatio in metalla.* 3. *In opus metalli.* 4. Banishment: (1) By interdiction of fire and water: (to which

abjuration of the realm in England had formerly a resemblance); (2) By deportation.

12. To capital punishments, confiscation, or forfeiture of goods, was incident: but this was remitted by the later emperors, in all crimes under the degree of treason.

13. Not capital punishments were, 1. Corporal: as whipping, fustigation, stigmatizing. 2. Taliation. 3. Relegation. 4. Infamy. 5. Pecuniary fines.

14. Imprisonment was no legal punishment among the Romans; and was not, regularly, allowed, unless the *reus* had *confessed* the crime with which he was charged. The Roman prison consisted of two parts: 1. *Robur*. 2. *Tullianum*. The keepers of the prison were three, called *triumviri*, or *tresviri capitales;* under whom was an officer, named *commentariensis*.

15. Punishments in England are, 1. Death; which, unless in treason, is usually inflicted by hanging. 2. Forfeiture of lands, or goods, or both; and corruption of blood. 3. Corporal, short of death: as whipping, setting in the pillory[1], or stocks. 4. Banishment; temporary or perpetual. 5. Imprisonment. 6. Pecuniary fines.

16. Public judgments among the Romans, were, I. *Lex Julia Majestatis*. II. *Lex Julia de Adulteriis*. III. *Lex Cornelia de Sicariis*. IV. *Lex Pompeia de Parricidiis*. V. *Lex Cornelia de Falsis*. VI. *Lex Julia de Vi publica et privata.*

[1] 56 George III. c. 138, abolishes the punishment of the pillory, except in the cases of perjury and subornation of perjury.

VII. *Lex Julia de Peculatu.* VIII. *Lex Fabia de Plagiariis.* IX. *Lex Julia Repetundarum, de Ambitu, de Annona, de Residuis.*

17. I. *Lex Julia Majestatis* was a law, promulged by Julius Cæsar, and again published, with additions, by Augustus, comprehending all the laws before enacted to punish transgressors against the state.

18. *Majestas* denotes the sovereign authority of a state, whether lodged in one person or more: whatever was attempted in violation of such authority was called *Crimen læsæ majestatis,* or treason.

19. Treason was further distinguished into, 1. *Crimen perduellionis.* 2. *Crimen læsæ majestatis in specie.*

20. *Perduellio* was, whatever was attempted directly against the being or safety of the republic, or of the prince, or his ministers.

21. *Læsa majestas in specie* was, whatever was attempted indirectly against the dignity and prerogative of the republic, or prince.

22. Lese majesty could not properly be committed *by* any but subjects; nor *against* any but those in whom the supreme power resided.

23. The punishment of perduellion was, 1. *Ultimum supplicium,* or natural death of the criminal. 2. Condemnation of his memory. 3. Forfeiture of his lands and goods; which forfeiture had relation to the time of the fact committed. 4. Exclusion of his sons from honours and succession. The punishment of lese majesty, specifically so called, was natural death, or deportation, or relegation; according to the circumstances of the crime.

24. In England, the law, by which those offences are defined that more immediately affect the person of the king, his crown, or dignity, and are distinguished by the name of High Treason, is the Statute of 25 Edward III. and that of 57 George III. c. 6. The species of high treasons, created by other statutes, are chiefly such as related to *papists,* and *relate* to the Protestant Succession.

25. The punishment of high treason, in males[1], is to be, 1. Drawn on a hurdle to the place of execution. 2. Hanged. 3. Beheaded. 4. Quartered. And in females to be drawn and hanged. In this judgment is implied, 1. Forfeiture of the offender's goods and lands; which forfeiture of *lands* has relation to the time of the fact committed. 2. Corruption of blood.

26. The provisions, made by the laws of England, to prevent oppression in the prosecution, and defect of certainty in the proof, of high treason; enumerated.

27. *Misprision of treason* is the knowledge and concealment of it, when committed by others; without any assent to the crime. The punishment of this offence, by the Civil Law, was the same as that of perduellion: but by the law of England is, 1. Forfeiture of goods. 2. Loss of the profits of lands during life. 3. Perpetual imprisonment.

28. Apostacy and heresy were considered, in the Roman Law, as treasons against Heaven; the prosecution of which, like that of treason against the state, might be commenced after the death of the offender, and judgment given against his memory.

[1] See 30 George III. c. 48; and 54 George III. c. 146.

29. The punishment of apostacy, in England, was formerly death: but, by the 9 and 10 Will. III. is now, for the first offence, incapacity; and for the second, incapacity, and three years imprisonment.

30. The punishment of heresy, by the Common Law of England, was death, in consequence of the writ *de hæretico comburendo:* but that writ is now abolished: and heresy in all its kinds, save that of maintaining there are more Gods than one, (which by the 9 and 10 of Will. III. c. 32, is liable to the same penalties as apostacy) is subjected to ecclesiastical correction only.

31. II. *Lex Julia de Adulteriis* was made to punish, 1. The crime of adultery. 2. The *crime against nature.* 3. *Incest.* 4. *Stuprum.*

32. Adultery, by the Julian Law, was the violation of a woman, who was married to another man.

33. The punishment of adultery was, 1. Relegation. 2. Confiscation of half the goods of both the parties. 3. Confiscation of half the *dos* of the adulteress.

34. By a constitution of the Emperor Constantine, the adulterer and the adulteress were both to be put to death. Justinian changed the punishment of death, on the part of the woman, to that of fustigation, together with confinement in a monastery; which confinement, unless the husband took her again within two years, was for life.

35. A father, who surprised his daughter in adultery, might kill the adulterer and his daughter too. A husband, who surprised his wife in adultery at his own house, or after three warnings, might kill the adulterer, but not his wife. In

England, the killing of an adulterer, taken in the act, by the husband, is manslaughter only, and not murder.

36. Adultery, as a public crime, is punishable, in England, in the Ecclesiastical Courts. In the Temporal Courts it is regarded as a private or civil injury; for which the husband has satisfaction in damages, by an action of trespass *vi et armis* against the adulterer.

37. The *crime against nature* was punished by the Civil, as it also is by the English, Laws, with death.

38. Incest between persons in the right line, was punished with deportation: between persons in the collateral line, the punishment was arbitrary. In England, this offence, like that of adultery, is punishable in the Ecclesiastical Courts.

39. *Stuprum* was the violation of a widow or virgin of character, without force.

40. The punishment of *stuprum*, in persons of rank and consideration, was the confiscation of half their goods: in meaner persons, it was corporal, with relegation.

41. The profession of a prostitute, though esteemed infamous among the Romans, was not obnoxious to legal censures.

42. III. *Lex Cornelia de Sicariis* was a law, enacted by L. Cornelius Sylla, the dictator, to punish, 1. The crime of homicide. 2. The crime called *veneficium*.

43. Homicide, or taking away the life of a human creature is, 1. Criminal. 2. Not criminal: which is, 1. Casual. 2. Necessary. 3. Culpable.

44. Criminal homicide, otherwise called murder, is the taking away the life of a human creature, with deliberation and malice: the punishment, by the Roman and the English Law, is death; and by the English Law, the execution is on the next day but one after the sentence, and the Court[1] directs that the prisoner be either hung in chains or buried within the precincts of the prison.

45. The wilful killing of a man's self was not considered in the Roman Law, as criminal: in the law of England, it is felony; and punished by ignominious burial, and forfeiture of goods.

46. Casual homicide is that, which is occasioned *per infortunium*, or by misadventure.

47. Necessary homicide is that, which is committed, 1. *Se defendendo*, or in self-defence. 2. For the prevention of some forcible crime.

48. Casual and necessary homicide were not obnoxious to punishment, by the Roman Law. In England, the killing of another *per infortunium*, or *se defendendo*, is called excusable homicide. The killing of another for the prevention of some forcible crime is justifiable homicide.

49. Culpable homicide is that, which is committed without malice, and through a sudden heat; which the law imputes to human infirmity. The punishment was arbitrary.

50. Culpable homicide, called in the law of England manslaughter, is felony; and is punished[2], at the discretion of the Court, with transportation, or imprisonment, or fine.

[1] See 2 and 3 William IV. c. 75. § 16.

[2] See 9 George IV. c. 31. § 9.

51. *Veneficium* is the crime of selling poison, or of practising magical arts and incantations; with a view of taking away the life of a human creature. The punishment was death.

52. Witchcraft and sorcery were formerly considered, in the law of England, as heresies and felonies; and were punished with death. But all prosecutions for these offences are now prohibited; and the pretenders to preternatural arts are punishable by imprisonment and the pillory.

53. IV. *Lex Pompeia de Parricidiis* was a law enacted, or rather restored, by Pompey the Great, against that species of criminal homicide, which was committed on parents and children, and on those who are *in the place* of parents and children. The punishment was sewing the criminal, together with certain other animals, in a sack, and throwing them alive into the sea.

54. V. *Lex Cornelia de Falsis* was enacted to punish the fraudulent suppression or imitation of truth, to the prejudice of another.

55. The *crimen falsi* might be committed, 1. By words. 2. By writing. 3. By deed.

56. The *crimen falsi* was committed by words, in the case of bearing false witness. Perjury, when committed in a Court of Justice, upon a capital accusation, was not comprehended under the law *de falsis;* but was included, as a species of assassination, under the law *de sicariis.* In England, perjury, and subornation of perjury, are, in all cases, punished by imprisonment, and, sometimes, transportation and the pillory.

57. The *crimen falsi* was committed by writing, in the case of making, altering, or suppressing a testament or other instrument. The fraudulent making, or altering, of a writing, to the prejudice of another, in England, is called forgery; the penalty[1] of which is now death in two cases, in all others transportation for life.

58. The *crimen falsi* was committed by deed, 1. In the case of counterfeiting or adulterating the public money. 2. A supposititious birth. 3. False weights and measures. 4. Selling or mortgaging the same thing to two persons in two several contracts. 5. Supporting the lawsuit of another by money, witnesses, or patronage; called, in the law of England, maintenance.

59. The ordinary punishment of the *crimen falsi* was deportation in freemen, and the *ultimum supplicium* in slaves: but in many cases it was arbitrary. In the cases of counterfeiting or adulterating the public money, (which in England is the crime of coining) and of a supposititious birth; the punishment was death: inflicted, in the former instance, by burning alive.

60. VI. *Lex Julia de Vi publica et privata,* was enacted to restrain public and private force. Public force was that which was committed with *arms,* in violation of the public peace: the punishment was deportation. Private force was committed without arms: and punished by confiscation of a third part of the estate of the offender, and infamy.

61. To public force was referred the *crimen raptus,* or the forcible abduction of a woman of

[1] See 2 and 3 William IV. c. 123.

character, for the sake of lust. The punishment was death in the ravisher, and his assistants; together with confiscation of the ravisher's estate.

62. Instances of public force, in England, are offences against the public peace: as, 1. Riotous assemblies, to the number of twelve: 2. The riotous destruction and demolition of property: the punishment is death. 3. Affrays. 4. Unlawful assemblies, routs, and riots. 5. Forcible entry and detainer. All punished by fine and imprisonment. 6. Going unusually armed: the penalty for which is forfeiture of the arms, and imprisonment.

63. The forcible abduction, and marriage or defilement, of an heiress, in England, is felony. The unlawful taking of any unmarried girl, under the age of sixteen years, out of the possession of and against the will of her parents or guardians, is a misdemeanor. Rape, or the carnal knowledge of a woman, forcibly, and against her consent; or of a woman child, under the *age* of *ten* years, even *with* her consent; is felony: punished with death. The carnal knowledge of a girl above the age of ten years and under the age of twelve years is a misdemeanor.

64. An instance of private force, in the law of England, is *champerty:* which is a bargain with the plaintiff or defendant in a suit, to have part of the land, debt, or other things sued for, if the party prevails at law; upon which the *champertor* carries on the suit at his own expense.

65. VII. *Lex Julia de Peculatu* was enacted, 1. To punish the crime of *peculatus.* 2. Sacrilege.

66. *Peculatus* is, 1. The embezzling of public money, belonging to the commonwealth, by one to

whose administration such money had not been committed. 2. The altering and removing of the books, containing the form and terrars of private lands. The punishment was, in magistrates and their accomplices, death: in private persons, deportation; and, sometimes, restitution of fourfold.

67. Sacrilege is the stealing of a *res sacra* or *religiosa* from a sacred or religious place. The punishment was death; but sometimes a lighter penalty was inflicted.

68. Embezzling the public money is punished, in England, by fine and imprisonment only. Sacrilege, or robbing the ornaments and goods of a church, was distinguished by the Common Law from other robberies; but by Statute it is put on the same footing with felonies[1].

69. VIII. *Lex Fabia de Plagiariis* was made to punish the crime, called *plagium*: by which was meant the fraudulent abduction, theft, or concealment of a freeman, or of a slave belonging to another. The punishment was formerly pecuniary: afterwards it was arbitrary, and, in some cases, capital.

70. *Plagium* is called, in the law of England, kidnapping; being the forcible stealing, or decoying away, of man, woman, or child, from their own country, and sending them into another. The penalty is fine, imprisonment, and other corporal punishment. The stealing of children under the age of ten years from their parents or guardians is felony.

71. IX. *Lex Julia Repetundarum, de Ambitu, de Annona, de Residuis*, was made to punish the

[1] See 5 and 6 William IV. c. 81.

several crimes, comprehended under those appellations.

72. *Crimen Repetundarum*, or bribery, was committed, when magistrates, or persons in any public office, received money, by themselves or their domestics, to do something *more* or *less* than their office obliged them to. The punishment was restitution of fourfold; and sometimes banishment, and confiscation of goods.

73. Bribery in England is, when a judge, or other person concerned in the administration of justice, takes a reward, to influence his behaviour in his office. The penalty is fine and imprisonment.

74. *Ambitus* is the unlawful buying and selling of any public office, or the procuring of honours and dignities by money or gifts. The punishment was a pecuniary fine, and infamy; and sometimes, deportation, and restitution of fourfold.

75. In England, the buying of offices, which concern the king's revenue, and the execution of justice; and corrupt elections and resignations in colleges, and other eleemosynary corporations; are restrained by certain statutes. The corrupt presentation of any one to an ecclesiastical benefice is called *Simony;* by which that turn is forfeited to the Crown.

76. *Crimen de Annona* (*fraudata*) is the abusing of the public markets or fairs, by which the price of provisions was made dearer. The punishment was a pecuniary fine, and other extraordinary animadversion.

77. Offences, relative to the buying of provisions, are chiefly comprehended, in England, under

the articles of, 1. Forestalling. 2. Regrating. 3. Engrossing: the penalty in all which is fine and imprisonment.

78. Monopolies, and combinations to keep up the price of merchandize, workmanship, and provisions, were punished, among the Romans, by banishment, and confiscation of goods. By the *Common* Law of England such combinations are conspiracies, and are punishable as misdemeanors.

79. *Crimen de Residuis* is retaining the public money, or converting it to other uses than those to which it was designed, by a magistrate to whose administration such money had been committed. The punishment was restitution of the *pecunia residua,* or money retained or converted, together with a third part of the sum over and above, and infamy.

80. The mal-administration of high officers in public trusts is usually punished, in England, by the method of parliamentary impeachment, with fine, banishment, and perpetual disability.

81. The punishments of the several crimes, which have here been mentioned, did not all descend from the laws by which those crimes were made public; but were, for the most part, appointed by the constitutions of the later emperors.

CHAPTER XIII.

OF THE FORM OF PUBLIC JUDGMENTS, OR THE COURSE OF PROCEEDING IN CRIMINAL CAUSES; AND OF JUDGMENTS OF THE PEOPLE; ACCORDING TO THE ROMAN LAW.

Heinecc. *A. R.* Lib. IV. Tit. 18, § 11—33.
Wood's *Inst. of the Civ. Law.* B. IV. ch. 4.
Esprit des Loix. Liv. VI. ch. 4. Liv. XI. ch. 18.
Pettingal's *Enquiry into the Use and Practice of Juries among the Greeks and Romans.* London, 1769.
Sigonii *de Judiciis,* II.
Wood's *Inst. of the Laws of England.* B. IV. ch. 5.
Blackstone's *Comm.* B. III. ch. 23. B. IV. ch. 21—32.
Principles of Penal Law. Ch. 25.
De Lolme's *Constitution of England.*
Cottu, *On the Spirit of the English Government.*

1. The power of judging criminal causes, among the Romans, which at first belonged to the kings and then to the consuls, was committed next to an extraordinary officer, appointed by commission for the prosecution of each crime, whose general name was *Quæstor Parricidii.*

2. Criminal causes were afterwards arranged under different heads, called *Quæstiones Perpetuæ;* and different prætors were created, to each of whom was assigned one or more of these questions, with power to judge the crimes depending on them, during the year of his magistracy.

3. Besides the prætor or quæstor, there were other persons, assistant to him in judgment; of whom the principal or chief was called *Judex Quæstionis;* and the rest were named *Judices Selecti.*

4. The regular number of judges was 450; which was again distributed into decuries, or committees of ten. Out of these a certain number was *selected,* for the trial of any particular crime; who sat together with the prætor, and gave their verdict, as jurors do in England.

5. A judicial enquiry into crimes might arise, 1. From inquisition. 2. Denunciation. 3. Accusation. In England, proceedings in courts of criminal jurisdiction are, 1. Summary, without the intervention of a jury. 2. Regular, with the intervention of a jury.

6. The constituent parts of a criminal cause, according to the form of public judgments, were, in order, these. I. *Vocatio in jus.* II. *Postulata facultas deferendi nomen.* III. *Delatio nominis, ejusque receptio.* IV. *Citatio rei.* V. *Sortitio judicum.* VI. *Actio prima sive accusatio.* VII. Proofs. VIII. *Defensio et laudatio rei.* IX. *Actio secunda sive comperendinatio.* X. *Missio judicum in consilium.* XI. Sentence. XII. Execution.

7. I. *Vocatio in jus* was a personal citation of the *reus,* or person accused, by which he was commanded to appear and answer to a crime, of which he was accused or suspected.

8. In great offences, or where the criminal had confessed the crime with which he was charged, the *reus* was sent to prison; and might be seized, even within his own house or walls. In small offences,

he was suffered to go at large, giving sureties for his appearance; or was committed to the custody of a soldier; or kept at the house of a magistrate.

9. In England, the beginning of the regular method of proceeding, in Courts of Criminal Jurisdiction, is by arrest: which is followed by commitment of the offender to prison; unless he is permitted[1] to find securities for his appearance, by giving bail.

10. II. *Postulata facultas deferendi nomen* was the accuser's asking of leave to *enter the name* of the criminal, together with the crime objected against him; on his own appearance and that of the *reus* before the quæstor or prætor.

11. Sometimes the *reus* would institute a cross accusation of the accuser, in order that he might be set aside as an infamous person. This cross accusation was called *Anticategoria.*

12. If more accusers than one appeared, a previous judgment was necessary, in order to determine which should be admitted to accuse. This previous judgment was called *Divinatio*[2].

13. III. *Delatio nominis* was the entering of the name of the *reus* on the roll of criminals, by the accuser; he having first taken the oath of calumny.

14. *Receptio nominis* was the admission of such name by the quæstor or prætor, in consequence of being asked by the accuser.

[1] See 7 George IV. c. 64.

[2] See the Oration of Cicero against Q. Cæcilius; in which the dispute is, whether he or Cæcilius ought to be admitted to accuse Verres, and which, for this reason, is intitled *Divinatio.*

15. The manner of accusing offenders in England is called their prosecution: which may be, 1. Upon a previous finding of the fact by a grand jury; either, (1) From their own knowledge, in the way of presentment; or, (2) upon a written accusation, in the form of an indictment. 2. Without such previous finding, (1) By information, at the suit of the king; (2) Formerly by appeal at the suit of the subject; but appeals of murder, felony, treason, or other offences, were abolished by 59 George III. c. 46.

16. IV. *Citatio rei* was the summoning of the *reus* to appear in court, in order to a trial, on a day, which had been before appointed by the prætor.

17. If on the day appointed the *reus* did not appear, banishment was inflicted on him, in his absence. If the accuser made default, the name of the person accused was struck from off the roll of criminals.

18. In England, when an offender is indicted in his absence, process is issued, to bring him into court: after which he is called upon by name to answer the matter of the indictment; which is termed his Arraignment. To this may be subsequent, 1. The standing mute of the prisoner. 2. His confession of the fact. 3. His pleading to the indictment.

19. The plea of a prisoner to the indictment is, 1. A plea to the jurisdiction. 2. A demurrer to the indictment. 3. A special plea in bar. 4. The general issue, Not Guilty.

20. V. *Sortitio judicum* was the chusing by lot of such a number out of the body of judges, as the law, on which the accusation was founded, had determined for the trial of the crime, objected to the *reus*.

21. In England, after issue joined, the usual method of trial is by jury: such jury being first impanelled by the sheriff, and *twelve* out of those whose names are returned on the panel, being chosen by lot.

22. When the number of judges was completed, the accuser or the *reus* had each the liberty of *rejecting* such of the persons selected as they disapproved; in like manner as jurors in England may be *challenged*, either on the part of the king or on that of the prisoner, as they appear, when called, to be sworn.

23. Challenges to the jury in England are, 1. To the whole panel, called challenges to the array. 2. To particular jurors, called challenges to the polls. Challenges to the polls are, 1. For cause. 2. Peremptory.

24. After rejection of any of the select judges, as many new ones were substituted in their place, as were wanting to complete the legal number. To this answers what is called in England striking a *tales*, or awarding a *tales de circumstantibus;* by which *such* men, as were summoned on the first panel, or are present in court, are joined to the other jurors, so as to complete the number of twelve.

25. VI. *Actio prima sive accusatio* was, what was urged by the accuser in a continued speech, in order to prove and aggravate the crime alleged against the *reus.*

26. VII. Proofs were principally had, 1. From witnesses: which were to be two in number at the least. In England, one positive witness is generally

sufficient to convict a prisoner, except in cases of treason and perjury. 2. Instruments or writings. 3. Confessions of slaves, belonging to the *reus;* which confessions were extorted by the rack. In some circumstances, the *reus* himself might be forced to a confession by torture: but no such proceeding is allowable by the laws of England.

27. VIII. *Defensio rei* was, what was urged by the advocates of the *reus,* in order to elude or extenuate the charge of the accuser.

28. *Laudatio rei* was, what was advanced by persons of authority and credit, in favour of the character of the *reus.*

29. In England, witnesses *for* the prisoner are examined upon oath, in like manner as witnesses *against* him: but a prisoner is not permitted to make his *full* defence by counsel, on a trial upon the general issue, in any cases of felony.

30. IX. *Actio secunda sive comperendinatio* was a second recitation of the cause, made by each party, after an adjournment of two days[1]. In some cases, such an adjournment was not allowed.

31. X. *Missio judicum in consilium* was the sending of the judges out, after the evidence on both sides was closed, in order to consult about their sentence. In England, after the proofs are summed up, the jury withdraw, unless the case be very clear, to consider of their verdict[2].

[1] See the six orations of Cicero against Verres; of which the first is called *Actio Prima,* and the other five are classed under the general name of *Actio Secunda.*

[2] The resemblance between the *Judices Selecti* of the Romans and English juries, in the several particulars mentioned in this

32. XI. Sentence was pronounced by the prætor, in conformity to the suffrages of the greater part of the judges: and was either, 1. *Ampliatio*, or an order for the rehearing of the cause, on a day appointed, for the sake of more ample information. 2. *Absolutio*, or a discharge of the *reus* from the same accuser, though not from the same accusation. 3. *Condemnatio*, or the pronouncing of him guilty.

33. In England, no verdict can be given by a jury, unless unanimous in their opinions. This verdict is sometimes, 1. Special; where, on the facts stated, they *doubt* the matter of law, and leave it to be determined by the Court: but is usually 2. General: (1) Not guilty; which discharges the

chapter, is so striking, as to render it extremely probable that the latter were derived from the former. Mr Justice Blackstone has taken notice of this circumstance*: but his observation, I conceive, would have been better placed, had he inserted it in his *fourth* book, where he treats of the method of proceeding in the Courts of Criminal Jurisdiction, instead of his *third*, where he considers the pursuit of remedies by action, in the case of private wrongs, or civil injuries. For in private judgments, or in the trials of civil causes, among the Romans, there was no *selection* of judges at all; but the prætor generally appointed *one* person only to examine the fact in question; as appears, among other proofs, from the phrase, *prætor dabat judicem* (in the singular number), and also from the formula used by him on this occasion, *C. Aquili, judex esto.* And indeed in the very instance, from Asconius on the *Verrinæ* of Cicero, to which the learned writer refers, the prosecution was not of a civil but a criminal nature; the accusation of Verres being instituted for a public crime, the *crimen peculatus;* which therefore could not be tried according to the form of private, but of public judgments.

* See Blackstone's *Comm.* B. III. ch. 23.

prisoner for ever of the accusation. (2) Guilty: upon which, or when the prisoner has *pleaded* guilty, he is said to be convicted.

34. The conviction of a prisoner, in England, is regularly followed by the judgment, or the pronouncing of the punishment expressly ordained by law. But judgment may be *arrested* by some intervening circumstance: or by the decision of the Court that the indictment[1] is defective in point of law.

35. XII. Execution of the sentence was called *Animadversio*, and was left to the care of the prætor. In England, it must be performed by the legal officer, and in the manner the law directs.

36. Execution of the sentence might be suspended, 1. By the intercession of the tribunes or consuls. 2. By appeal.

37. After judgment of death, or of outlawry for a capital offence, in England, the attainder of a criminal commences. But judgment, and its consequences, may be avoided, 1. By falsifying or reversing the judgment. 2. By reprieve or pardon.

II.

Heinecc. *A. R.* Lib. IV. Tit. 18. § 3. 34—35.	Blackstone's *Comm.* B. IV. ch. 10. 31.
Sigonii *de Judiciis*, III.	*Esprit des Loix*. Liv. XII. ch. 19.

38. BESIDES public judgments, there were also judgments of the people, called *Judicia populi;* which

[1] See Prop. 19. 2.

were held by the Romans, assembled at their *Comitia Centuriata*, or *Tributa*, and related both to private and public causes[1].

39. The constituent parts of a cause, whether civil or criminal, when heard before the Roman people, were, in order, these. I. *Diei dictio.* II. *Citatio rei.* III. *Accusatio*, IV. *Promulgatio.* V. *Defensio rei.* VI. *Populi vel plebis suffragia.*

40. *Diei dictio* was the notice given by a magistrate, that he intended to impeach a certain citizen, (whom he mentioned by name) of a certain crime, before the people, on a certain day.

41. *Citatio rei* was the summoning of the *reus* to appear, according to appointment, on a day prefixed. If, through contumacy or consciousness of guilt, the *reus* was absent; an arbitrary punishment was imposed on him by the magistrate, who meant to accuse him.

42. *Accusatio* was the charge brought against the *reus* before the people, and repeated thrice. To this was added an intimation, called *anquisitio*, of the mulct or punishment intended, which was assigned by the accusing magistrate at his discretion.

43. *Promulgatio* was the publishing of the accusation, together with the mulct or punishment proposed, on three successive market days, for the information of the people.

44. *Defensio rei* was what was urged by the *reus*, or by his advocates, after the time of promul-

[1] See the account of the accusation of P. Scipio Africanus before the Roman people, as related by Livy, in the 38th Book of his History; which is illustrated not a little from this part of the Civil Law.

gation was expired, in order to elude or extenuate the crime alleged against him. After which a day was fixed, on which the people were to assemble, in order to give their judgment.

45. *Populi vel plebis suffragia* were the votes of the people or of the plebeians, in the *Comitia centuriata*, or *Tributa;* and given *per tabellas*, in the manner used in passing a law: by a majority of which the *reus* was acquitted or condemned.

46. To these judgments of the people, among the Romans, the trial, in England, of great offenders, before the Lords, in consequence of a parliamentary impeachment by the Commons, is, in some respects, similar.

APPENDIX.

STATUTA

QUÆDAM

ACADEMIÆ CANTABRIGIENSIS.

No. I.

CAP. XII.

DE LEGUM *STUDIOSIS*.

QUI a primo in academiam adventu *legibus* operam dabit, primum annum integrum *institutionum* lectioni domi suæ impendat; deinde quinquennium totum Publicum Juris Professorem audiat. Respondebit publice semel Professori, aut alicui Doctori ejusdem facultatis, antequam fiat Baccalaureus Juris. Qui fuit ante Baccalaureus Artium, quatuor annorum studio poterit Juris esse Baccalaureus, si ordine præscripto responderit.

CAP. XIII.

DE LEGUM BACCALAUREIS.

HIC etiam Regium in Jure Professorem audiat quinquennium. Respondebit hoc tempore bis in suis scholis, opponet semel; et cooptabitur Doctor.

Magister Artium, septennium dans operam *legibus*, et cæteris perfunctis quæ hic requiruntur, poterit cooptari inter Legum Doctores.

CAP. XIV.

DE LEGUM DOCTORIBUS.

DOCTOR Legum mox a Doctoratu dabit operam legibus *Angliæ;* ut non sit imperitus earum legum quas habet sua patria, et differentias exteri patriique juris noscat.

No. II.

CAP. XLII.

DE CANCELLARII OFFICIO.

CANCELLARIUS potestatem habebit ad *omnes* omnium scholasticorum atque etiam eorum famulorum *controversias*, summarie, atque sine ulla juris solennitate præter illam quam nos præscribimus[1], secundum Jus Civile et eorum privilegia et consuetudines, tum audiendas tum dirimendas: ad congregationes graduatorum et scholasticorum convocandas: ad homines dignos gradibus scholasticis ornandos, qui omnia munera scholastica, his contenta statutis, expleverint; et ad indignos rejiciendos ab iisdem et repellendos: ad omnes eorum violatores puniendos: ad providendum prætcrea ut singuli academiæ ministri in suo officio se contineant; ignavos, grassatores, rei suæ dissipatores, contumaces, nec obedientes, suspensione graduum, carcere, aut alio leviore supplicio, *judicio suo*, castigandos. Non licebit tamen Cancellario aliquem scholarem exilio mulctare[2], aut aliquem pileatorum aut præfectorum col-

[1] Some copies read *præscribemus.*

[2] *In the stat. de* Cancellarii officio *given in the 1st of Eliz. and in the 42nd and 45th of her second body of Statutes, the Chancellor is restrained from inflicting certain punishments without the assent of the Heads of Colleges. It has been urged that this*

legiorum incarcerare, absque consensu majoris partis præfectorum collegiorum. Quicquid statutis nostris, vel academiæ[1], Cancellario faciendum attribuitur, in ejus absentia, hoc idem a Procancellario fiat. Eidem Cancellario, cum consensu totius academiæ, licebit

this restriction establishes a new jurisdiction, distinct from the Chancellor's Court. But this opinion is neither supported by the Statutes nor the practice of the University. It is true that, in certain cases, the assent of the Heads of Colleges is necessary to the judgment. Yet, in all these cases, the Chancellor is the sole judge, the proceedings are regulated by him, and the sentence is his. The first of the above Statutes empowers the Chancellor to inflict certain punishments, mentioned in that Statute, Judicio suo et assensu præfectorum ædium. *The second empowers him to inflict the same punishments* judicio suo; *but restrains him from banishing a scholar, &c.* absque consensu majoris partis præfectorum collegiorum. *The third directs the Chancellor to banish, for a certain offence, with their assent,* Cancellarii jussu cum assensu majoris partis præfectorum collegiorum. *In these Statutes the Chancellor alone is spoken of as the judge, the Heads of Colleges are not considered as making a part of the Court. It is never said* jussu *or* judicio Cancellarii et præfectorum; *but* Cancellarii jussu *or* judicio cum assensu præfectorum.

This construction of the Statutes is confirmed by the practice of the University, which, in this respect, appears to have been uniform. On a late application to the Court of King's Bench for a mandamus, several precedents were cited, on the part of the University, shewing that causes which require the assent of the Heads of Colleges have been heard in the Chancellor's Court, and it did not appear from a single case, that any such cause had been tried and determined before a different tribunal.

The rule for a mandamus came on to be argued several times. The judges delivered their opinions at great length, and unanimously decided in favour of the University.

See Durnford and East's Reports, Mich. Term, 1794.
Rex, v. *Chancellor of Cambridge.*

[1] *Vel academiæ;* that is, by the *old* Statutes of the University, before those given by Q. Elizabeth.

nova statuta, ad eruditionis amplificationem et decori atque honesti conservationem inter scholasticos habendam, sancire; sic ut ea his decretis nostris nihil detrahant aut officiant[2].

[2] It hath been said that the 42d Statute, *de Cancellarii officio,* gives a right to interpose in *criminal* matters, or matters relating to correction and discipline *only:* and that from the power committed in this Statute to the Chancellor, of punishing contumacy and some other offences *judicio suo;* as also from *immediate imprisonment* being one of the punishments allowed; (which, it has been pretended, may be executed *before* there *can* be an appeal) it necessarily follows, that the jurisdiction of the Chancellor is *final, in the first instance.* But it hath been answered, with equal truth and sagacity, that the very first clause, *Cancellarius potestatem habebit ad* omnes—*Scholasticorum*—*Controversias*—Secundum Jus Civile *et eorum privilegia et consuetudines, tum audiendas tum dirimendas*—is alone sufficient to prove, that the administration of *civil* as well as *criminal* justice is here included. 2dly. That the words *judicio suo* mean no more, than that in causes of *less moment,* and towards offenders of *inferior rank,* the Chancellor may proceed by his sole judgment, or *single authority,* without the concurrence of the Heads of Colleges: or, that he may inflict on offenders *which* of the several censures mentioned in the statute—*Suspensio graduum, carcere, aut alio leviore supplicio*—he shall think fit, *at his discretion:* but by no art of construction can be made to contain the sense of *final determination.* 3dly. That it is not true, there can be no appeal from a sentence of *imprisonment,* because such sentence is to be executed *immediately;* for an appeal may be made *apud acta**, as in other Ecclesiastical Courts, which may suspend the execution. Lastly, that, even supposing the 42d Statute to relate *merely* to criminal causes, it will not follow, from *no mention* being there made of an appeal from the Chancellor's sentence, that the *omission* in such a case amounts to a *prohibition,* and that appeals in criminal causes

* See ch. IX. pr. 47. and ch. XI. pr. 28. 31. of the Third Book of this Analysis. The words of the Civil Law are express: *Si* apud acta *quis appellaverit, satis erit si dicat,* appello. D. 49. 1, 2.

CAP. L.

DE ORDINATIONIBUS COLLEGIIS PRÆSCRIPTIS.

STATUTA omnia, compositiones et consuetudines, quæ Scripturis Sacris, Institutis Nostris, aut Istis Statutis[1] adversari videbuntur, abrogata et rescissa sunto; reliquis suo robore permansuris.

Si quid dubii vel ambigui in istis statutis et sanctionibus nostris oriatur; id per Cancellarium et majorem partem præfectorum collegiorum explicabitur et determinabitur: quorum determinationi et interpretationi reliquos omnes cedere volumus.

are not allowed by the Statutes of the University: for the powers given to the Chancellor are still to be exercised, in conformity to the *privileges* and *customs* of the University; and the same clause, which impowers the Chancellor to judge *omnes controversias scholasticorum,* requires him also to judge *secundum Jus Civile:* now the *Civil Law,* it is certain*, allows appeals in *all* causes, criminal as well as civil.

[1] *Istis Statutis;* that is, the *New* Statutes of Q. Elizabeth.

* See the note on ch. x. pr. 32. of the Third Book of this Analysis.

No. III.

CAP. XLVIII.

DE CAUSIS FORENSIBUS.

OMNES causæ et lites, quæ ad Universitatis notionem pertinent, tam *Procancellarii* quam *Commissarii* judicio subjiciantur: nisi procuratores vel taxatores academiæ, aut eorum aliquis, vel magister artium, aut qui supra illum fuerit, alter litigantium sit: tunc enim *Procancellarii solius* erit jurisdictio; nisi in nundinis Sturbrigiensibus, et iis quæ ad festum Sancti Johannis Baptistæ apud Barnwell, tenentur. Finem autem accipiant *intra triduum*, si fieri potest; omni juris solennitate semota.

A Sententia Commissarii ad *Procancellarium appellabitur*, intra viginti quatuor horas post latam sententiam. A *Procancellario* autem, sive lis coram eo *cæpta* sit, sive per appellationem ad eum *devoluta*, ad *Universitatem* provocatio, fiet, intra triduum a tempore latæ sententiæ, et non post: suamque appellationem *intimabit* appellans *alteri procuratorum*, intra triduum latæ sententiæ. Ille vero statim, nomine academiæ, judici *a quo inhibebit*, ne quid, pendente appellatione, *attentare* vel innovare præsumat; prius tamen duobus solidis, honorarii loco, ab appellante acceptis; nec non viginti solidis apud eum depositis appellanti restituendis, si justam fovisse causam probetur; vel in usum academiæ convertendis, si temere appellasse convincatur, aut si post *datos judices* a persecutione cessaverit, vel culpa sua cognitio differatur. Causæ appellationem ad Universitatem *ultra decem dies*, si fieri potest, post datos judices, non protrahantur. Nec *secunda appellatio* omnino admittatur.

Judices Delegati, tres ad minimum, nec plures quam quinque, pro qualitate causæ in omni appellatione *dabuntur;* et sententiæ majoris partis illorum standum erit. Potestas autem *nominandi* Judices sit penes *quinque* illos viros qui pro *Capite* illius anni constituti sunt, et *duos Procuratores*. Et qui a majore parte istorum nominati fuerint, ad Regentes et non Regentes deferentur, suffragiis suis *eligendi*, si placent eis: alioqui, mutatis uno vel altero, alii, eorum loco per dictos *Septemviros* surrogati, proponentur eligendi: et si hi quoque displicent, similiter tertio fiet. Quod si nec tertio loco positi eligantur, licebit dictis Septemviris, aut eorum majori parti, pro illa vice tantum, Delegatos Judices eligere et dare. Et si major pars Septemvirorum, vel in *nominandis* Judicibus, vel in *eligendis* illis, (quando electio ad eos devolvitur) non conveniat; tunc plures numero prævalebunt, licet majorem partem vel æquam, habita ratione totius numeri, non efficiant[1].

[1] It hath been asserted, that the 48th Statute, *De Causis Forensibus*, (where an appeal from the sentence, both of the Commissary and the Vice-Chancellor, is expressly given, and the manner of appealing is prescribed) relates to *civil* causes

only, in which two parties are litigant*. But here again, the words in the beginning of the Statute, never afterwards restrained or limited,—*Omnes Causæ et Lites, quæ ad Universitatis notionem pertinent, tam Procancellarii quam Commissarii judicio subjiciantur*—are as *general* as any words can be, so as to comprehend trials of *every sort:* although it is not to be wondered, that the same critics, who would confine *omnes Controversias* in the 42d Statute to *criminal* causes, should also confine *omnes Causæ et Lites* in the 48th statute to *civil* causes only. Secondly, the appeal *from the Commissary to the Vice-Chancellor* is given in the same clause, and in the same manner, with the appeal *from the Vice-Chancellor to the delegates:* and the words of the *Commissary's Patent* extend as well to causes of correction and censure, as to civil causes. Now there can be no doubt, but that an appeal lies *from the Commissary to the Vice-Chancellor* in *all* cases.

The mistake on this subject seems to have arisen, from imagining that the *express* authority of Statute is required, to make good the claim to appeals; whereas the right stands entirely on the *nature of University-Jurisdiction:* in consequence of which there hath been an immemorial *practice* of appealing; supposed indeed and admitted in both the *old* and *new* statutes, and authorized by the prescription of various rules, for the exercises of it; but neither expressly commanded, nor prohibited in either.

See an excellent pamphlet, (from whence the explanations of this Statute, *De causis Forensibus,* as also that of Statute the 42d, *De Cancellarii Officio,* inserted in the Appendix No. II. has been extracted) intitled, *The Opinion of an eminent Lawyer concerning the Right of Appeal from the Vice-Chancellor of Cambridge. By a Fellow of a College.*

* The *title* of this Statute is certainly not sufficient to support such an assertion: at least if the opinion of the celebrated *Vinnius,* who is surely a competent judge on this occasion, be at all regarded; and who has plainly declared, that, in *his* conception, *Causæ Forenses* implied something *more* than civil causes merely. That learned civilian, in his useful work, intitled *Partitiones Juris Civilis,* (Lib. III. Chap. 17.) being led by his subject to speak of the *Office of Assessors,* informs us, that it consists, among other particulars, *in cognitionibus; id est,* as he himself explains his meaning, *in Causarum Forensium Quæstionibus et Disceptationibus, Sive Civiles sint et Pecuniariæ, Sive Publicæ et Criminales.*

No. IV.

SENATUS-CONSULTUM SIVE GRATIA.

13 Feb. 1593.

Cum Academiæ Statuto *De Causis Forensibus* cautum sit, ut omnes lites, si fieri possit, *intra triduum* terminentur, nec causæ appellationum *ultra decem dies*, si fieri itidem possit, post datos Judices, protrahantur: usu autem jam compertum sit, quorundam *Malitia* factum esse, ut multæ appellationes non tam bona fide quam vexandorum adversariorum gratia ab hominibus litigiosis interpositæ fuerint: idcirco, ut huic incommodo in posterum omnino subveniatur, placet vobis, ut unanimi Procancellarii, Doctorum, Magistrorum Regentium, et Non-Regentium, auctoritate statutum et decretum sit, ut, in omni deinceps appellatione, pars appellans, una cum advocato, patrono et procuratore suo, statim post appellationem sive a Commissario sive a Procancellario factam, præstet *Juramentum Corporale* coram Judice *a quo*, quod *in conscientia sua justam habeat causam appellandi:* præterea etiam, ut, appellatione a Procancellario ad Academiam facta, utraque pars, tam appellans quam appellata[1], et utriusque etiam

[1] By the *pars appellata* here is not meant the *judex a quo,* but the party who has got a sentence in his favour. After an

partis advocatus, patronus et procurator, similiter juramentum præstent corporale, quod *neque directe, neque indirecte, neque per se neque per alium quempiam, Septemviros, apud quos potestas est Delegatos Judices nominandi solicitent ad assignandum aliquem Delegatum, sed ipsorum arbitrio talem nominationem libere permittent.* Et ut quæcunque appellationes deinceps in quibuscunque Forensibus Controversiis, sive ab *Interlocutoria Sententia* sive *Definitiva,* interponentur, eas *intra quadraginta dies,* proxime post inhibitionem factam numerandos, quocunque impedimento non obstante, Delegati Judices, virtute juramenti sui academiæ præstiti, terminare teneantur: nisi forte per appellantem steterit hujusmodi dilatio; quo in casu, irrita sit appellatio et pro *deserta* habeatur.—Et, ut hoc Decretum Vestrum pro Statuto habeatur, et in libris procuratorum infra decem dies immediate sequentes inscribatur?

an appeal, the two parties in the cause, instead of being called *actor* and *reus,* are now denominated *pars appellans* and *pars appellata.* See Oughton's *Ordo Judiciorum,* Tit. 301. § 2.

No. V.

SENATUS CONSULTUM SIVE GRATIA.

24 Oct. 1609.

Cum Statutis Academiæ nostræ cautum sit, ut omnes causæ in aliqua curia Universitatis motæ, omni Juris solennitate semota et sola facti veritate inspecta, debite terminentur *intra triduum*, si commode fieri possit; quæ quidem Statuta (inter alia) quilibet advocatus, procurator, et alii omnes sese ad postulandum gerentes in Curiis prædictis, virtute juramenti stricte tenentur observare: quibus tamen non obstantibus, jampridem omnes pene lites, coram Procancellario et Commissario Universitatis nostræ inceptæ, potius in triennium quam triduum prorogantur; in manifestam privilegiorum et Statutorum nostrorum violationem, honoris et jurisdictionis Academiæ scandalum et opprobrium, et litigantium vexationem et dispendium: placet itaque vobis, ut subsequens *ordo* in omnibus et singulis causis posthac in Curiis Universitatis motis seu movendis stricte observetur? viz.

Imprimis arctetur reus, si possit apprehendi; si non possit, fiat *citatio* peremptoria *viis et modis*. Reo capto, seu *bonis suis*, ex *primo decreto*, salva custodia custodiatur, donec *fidem jubeat* coram Academiæ Registrario vel ejus deputato, se compariturum proximo *die juridico* ex tunc sequenti, et sic postea quolibet, etc, reo autem non comparente, statim luant *Fidejussores* sine favore.

Insuper, *juxta tenorem Statutorum Academiæ*[1] *nostræ*, principales personæ factum ipsum per se proponant; viz. *actor* per se suam *actionem*, et *reus* suam *defensionem:* nec *defensores* vel *procuratores* admittantur pro iisdem, nisi adversa valetudine vel alia legitima causa per dominum approbanda sint detenti, quo minus in judicio sui præsentiam poterunt exhibere: de quibus in principio, coram Domino Procancellario vel Commissario vel Delegatis Judicibus, fidem faciat (*lege* faciant) juramento; quo præstito, et causa utrinque declarata, et non ante, admittantur.

1. His omnibus sic ut præcipitur factis et observatis, primo die juridico detur materia, sive facti *declaratio;* fiat etiam *litis contestatio;* et præstet

[1] The words *juxta tenorem Statutorum Academiæ* refer to the *old* Statutes of the University, such as obtained before those given by Queen Elizabeth in the year 1570: which Old Statutes, it is apprehended are *still* in force, so far as they do not *detrahere aut officere aut adversari* those of the Queen. The passages alluded to out of the Old Statutes are: Principales personæ factum ipsum per se proponant: actor, viz. primo per se suam proponat actionem, reus vero per se suam afferat defensionem. *De advocatis in auditione causarum.* Again, Nec defensores nec procuratores coram Cancellario vel ejus Commissario admittantur pro iisdem, nisi personæ citatæ adversa valetudine seu alia legitima causa sint detentæ, quo minus in judicium sui præsentiam poterunt exhibere: de quo in principio coram Cancellario vel ejus Commissariis fidem faciant juramento: quo præstito, admittantur defensores seu procuratores, juxta Consuetudines et Statuta Universitatis, in litem processuri. *De defensoribus et procuratoribus litigantium.*

reus juramentum *de fideliter respondendo;* et moneatur ad subeundum examen intra triduum: (nisi causæ sint leviores et ordinariæ; in quibus judex potest statim tam partes principales quam testes, si quos præsentes habeat, *publice* interrogare et examinare de veritate facti; et, omni solennitate prorsus semota, causam statim finaliter determinare.) Sed utcunque triduo elapso, vel antea si fieri possit, habeat actor *copiam responsi,* ut videat an opus habeat ulteriori probatione; et sciat, quod ultra ei faciendum habeat etiam *ad probandum in proximum:* et post triduum, etiam *compulsorium pro testibus.*

2. Secundo die juridico[1] veniat actor paratus *ad probandum;* et *testes* suos *producat* si quos habeat. Testes judex, in levioribus et ordinariis causis, potest, ut supra, *publice* interrogare de veritate materiæ sive *allegationis;* et statim causam finaliter determinare: sin causa longior sit, et altiorem examinationem requirat, habeat reus biduum pro *in-*

[1] These regulations are founded on the practice of the Ecclesiastical Courts, in which the proceedings are by private examination of witnesses upon allegations and interrogatories, and subsequent publication. But, the Grace allows the Chancellor, when the cause is *levior et ordinaria,* to proceed in a less dilatory way, and to examine witnesses publicly. Now whether the cause is *levior et ordinaria,* or, *longior et altiorem examinationem requirens,* is left to the discretion of the judge. And Vice-Chancellors, by virtue of this discretionary power, have of late constantly proceeded summarily, and have heard witnesses examined *vivâ voce,* which is, at least, as effectual and expeditious a way of coming at the truth as the other.

See *The proceedings in the Court of Delegates on the Appeal of William Frend, M. A. &c. Cambridge,* 1793.

terrogatoriis; et intra principium tertii diei et diem proximum juridicum, examinentur testes tam super materia originali actoris quam super interrogatoriis per reum datis.

3. Tertio die juridico *publicentur dicta testium,* et *assignetur ad sententiam, in proximum;* et proximo feratur sententia, nisi reus velit *excipere.* Si velit, detur reo proximus *ad excipiendum:* quo die adveniente, *respondeat* actor, ut supra reus actori, et præstet juramentum, et subeat examen, ut supra: et reo detur *terminus ad probandum in proximum;* et fiat, ut supra actori.

4. Quarto die producantur testes rei si quos habeat; qui juramento suscepto moneantur examinari citra proximum: reliquaque fiant per judicem, vel in publica testium examinatione, vel in concedendis alteri interrogatoriis, quæ secundo die juridico fiebant de testibus actoris.

5. Quinto die publicentur dicta testium* rei, assignetur ad sententiam proximo, et *ad informandum interim.*

6. Sexto die feratur sententia.

7. Septimo et ultimo, nisi interim ab altera parte *appellatum fuerit,* mandetur sententia *executioni.*

Placet etiam vobis, ut quilibet advocatus, procurator sive causarum defensor, neenon quilibet Officiarius Curiarum Academiæ nostræ, virtute juramenti

* It is very observable, that the word, *testes,* is never here used in the singular number, but always in the plural; agreeably to the Civil Law, which requires *two* witnesses at least, to make proof.

sui corporalis per eorum quemlibet præstandi, præmissa omnia et singula stricte teneantur observare, priusquam in ullis causis in posterum in dictis Curiis movendis admittantur: et ut iste *ordo* et hæc concessio vestra pro Statuto habeatur, et in libris procuratorum infra decem dies jam proxime sequentes inscribatur?

No. VI.

JURAMENTUM PROCURATORUM ET ADVOCATORUM IN CONSISTORIO.

Ego A. B. ad ista Sancta Dei Evangelia per me corporaliter tacta juro, quod Statuta, privilegia et consuetudines Universitatis Cantabrigiæ approbatas pro posse meo fideliter observabo: Ministros dictæ Universitatis honorifice tractabo: jurisdictionem ejusdem nullo modo impediam, nec impedire volentibus seu volenti consilium vel auxilium præstabo: cæteris Statutis, de advocatis mentionem facientibus, in suo robore duraturis.

Jurabis etiam, quod omnia et singula, contenta in Statuto per Universitatem facto vicesimo quarto die Octobris Anno Domini 1609, pro posse tuo observabis: ita te Deus adjuvet etc.

No. VII.

FORMS OF SUPPLICATS, &c. FOR THE DEGREES OF BACHELOR AND DOCTOR OF LAWS.

LL. B.

—— *Coll.* —— *Mens.* —— *Ann.*

1. SUPPLICAT Reverentiis Vestris A. B. ut studium sex annorum in Jure Civili, in quibus ordinarias lectiones audiverit (licet non omnino secundum formam statuti) una cum omnibus responsionibus, cæterisque exercitiis per Statuta Regia requisitis, sufficiat ei ad intrandum in eodem jure.

C. D. *Prælector.*

At the time this *supplicat* is offered to the *Caput* of the University Senate, there must also be presented, in writing, under the hand and seal of the Master of the College concerned, or his deputy, a form to the following effect:

—— *Coll.* —— *Month.* —— *Year.*

"A. B. was admitted into this College on the ——day of——, in the year——; has resided the greater part of nine several terms; and has continued a Member of the College for six years complete, or to the present time.

E. F. *Master*, or *President*,
or *Locum Tenens Custodis.*
C. D. *Prælector.*

If A. B. has been a Member of two Colleges, the form may be to the following effect:

—— *Coll.* —— *Month.* —— *Year.*

"A. B. was admitted into this College on the —— day of ——, in the year ——; has resided the greater part of —— several terms, and continued a Member to the present time, or to the —— day of —— in the year ——."

E. F. *Master*, or *President*,
or *Locum Tenens Custodis.*
C. D. *Prælector.*

And in compliance with a Grace of the Senate a Certificate must also be presented to the Caput, under the hand of the Regius Professor of the Faculty, that the Student has attended his Lectures during three terms.

LL. D.

2. Supplicat Reverentiis Vestris A. B. ut studium quinque annorum post Gradum Baccalaureatus in Jure Civili susceptum, [*or, if a Master*[1] *of Arts*, studium septem annorum, postquam Rexerit in Artibus,] in quibus ordinarias lectiones audiverit, (licet non omnino secundum formam Statuti) una cum omnibus oppositionibus, responsionibus, cæterisque exercitiis per Statuta Regia requisitis, sufficiat ei ad incipiendum in eodem jure.

[1] If a Master of Arts desires to be admitted LL.D., he must have declared himself a Student of the Civil Law to the Vice-Chancellor in the presence of the Registrary.

A CAUTION GRACE.

3. Cum A. B. unicam oppositionem [*vel* unicam responsionem; *vel* unicam oppositionem et unicam responsionem; *vel* duas responsiones; *vel* unicam oppositionem et duas responsiones] præstare teneatur, antequam admitti possit ad Gradum Doctoratus in Jure Civili; placeat vobis, ut dictum exercitium [*vel* dicta exercitia] differatur [*vel* differantur] in terminum proxime sequentem, tunc temporis peragendum vel peragenda, sub pœna viginti solidorum; *vel* viginti quatuor librarum et decem solidorum; *vel* viginti quinque librarum et decem solidorum; *vel* quadraginta et novem librarum *vel* quinquaginta librarum cistæ communi applicandorum [*vel* applicandarum]; atque ut ipse interea vel in hac vel in alia Congregatione admissionem suam obtineat.

This Caution Grace (not the *supplicat,* which must always be signed by the College-Lecturer, and, as I apprehend, by him *only*) must be signed by nine Heads of Colleges, and also by the greater part of the Faculty, present in the University.

AN INDEX

TO THE

ANALYSIS AND APPENDIX.

AN INDEX

TO THE

ANALYSIS AND APPENDIX.

A.

B.

K.

L.

N.

T.

V. U.

INDEX TO STATUTES

TO WHICH REFERENCE IS MADE.

www.ingramcontent.com/pod-product-compliance
Lightning Source LLC
LaVergne TN
LVHW091527200926
848483LV00002B/329
* 9 7 8 1 5 8 4 7 7 8 9 0 5 *